A Manual of the Sub-Kingdom Protozoa

Joseph Reay Greene

BIBLIOBAZAAR

A

MANUAL

OF THE

SUB-KINGDOM

PROTOZOA.

WITH A GENERAL INTRODUCTION ON

THE PRINCIPLES OF ZOOLOGY.

BY

JOSEPH REAY GREENE, B.A.

PROFESSOR OF NATURAL HISTORY IN THE QUEEN'S COLLEGE, CORK,
&c. &c.

NEW EDITION.

LONDON:

LONGMAN, GREEN, LONGMAN, ROBERTS, & GREEN.

1863.

PREFACE.

IT has been the Author's aim to embody, in the present Manual, a succinct *résumé* of what is known concerning those humbler forms of animal life which constitute the department of Protozoa: and in so doing, he has, as much as possible, sought to interpret the observations of others by the light which he has gained from the results of his own investigations.

A list of the more important memoirs on the Protozoa has been appended to the general account of these animals, in the hope that it may prove useful to those advanced students who may be desirous of entering on their special study.

Titles are affixed to the numbered paragraphs, both with a view to facilitate reference, and also to guide the junior student in selecting those branches of the subject, with which, on a first perusal, it is most desirable that he should be made familiar. It will be found, however, that the general plan of the work is independent of these artificial divisions.

In treating of the classification of the Protozoa, it will be seen that the expressions, *class, order, family*, and *genus,* are not here made use of. To these terms a definite meaning is, or ought to be, always attached, and it would, therefore, be premature to apply them to the subdivisions of the Protozoa; the natural groups into which this department is resolvable not having been yet determined with absolute certainty.

Since the present work is the first of a series of similar treatises, on the several departments of the Animal Kingdom, it has been deemed necessary to prefix thereto a brief introduction on the general principles of zoological science.

QUEEN'S COLLEGE, CORK,
May, 1859.

CONTENTS.

▲ 4

GENERAL INTRODUCTION.

ON THE PRINCIPLES OF ZOOLOGY.

BIOLOGY is that branch of scientific inquiry which undertakes to investigate the nature and relations of living bodies. It is the object of this science, by a careful study of the several beings of which the organic world is composed, to arrive at a knowledge of those general "laws" by which it is governed.

Every living being may be regarded from two points of view, which it is necessary to distinguish clearly from one another. The first of these exhibits to us living beings as possessing definite forms, which, in most instances, are found to be made up of a number of dissimilar parts or *organs ;* while the second takes cognisance of the vital actions or *functions* which those organs perform. That department of Biology which determines the former is termed *Morphology ;* that which investigates the latter *Physiology.* Hence the *nature* of living beings is two-fold — *Morpho-logical* and *Physiological.*

The *relations* of living beings may, in like manner, be viewed under two distinct aspects, namely:

1. Their relations to one another, *i. e.* their mutual or subjective relations.

2. Their relations to the conditions in which they are placed, *i. e.* their external or objective relations.

We endeavour to express our appreciation of the first kind of relations in our attempts to frame a natural *Classification;* whilst our knowledge of the second is involved in a statement of those facts from which, it is hoped, we may be enabled to deduce the laws of *Distribution.*

But what are the characters of living beings, and how may they be distinguished from the members of the inorganic world? This question presents itself for solution at the outset of our inquiries, since it is desirable to determine the limits of the region which we have undertaken to explore.

To frame a definition of life, is, however, impossible, this agent being only known to us by its effects.[1] When the so-called vital principle is associated with matter, as in a living body, we invariably observe that it confers upon the latter a tendency to pass through a series of changes.

Such changes are always definite and follow one another in a determinate order. This is the most general and characteristic feature of living beings, since matter, of itself, if unacted on from without, is incapable of undergoing any change.

Other peculiarities, of minor importance, distinguish living from inorganic bodies. Of these, the principal have reference to *external form, internal structure, chemical constitution,* and *mode of increase.*

1. External form. — The figure of living beings is always more or less rounded, being bounded by convex surfaces. That of inorganic bodies, on the contrary, is either indefinite (amorphous), or, if regular (crystalline), is, with very few exceptions, bounded by angles and right lines.

2. Internal structure. — The structure of a mineral body, provided it be pure and unmixed with any other substance, is altogether *homogeneous,* consisting throughout of an aggregation of similar particles. Such a body, therefore, cannot properly be said to possess any structure whatsoever, whereas the body of a living being usually consists of several parts, distinct from one another, which, again, in their turn, are seen to be composed of more minute constituents or tissues, these last being yet again resolvable into certain ultimate elementary components. Hence their structure is said to be *heterogeneous,* and the expression organised bodies has come to be synony-

mous with living beings. There are, however, some organisms of exceedingly simple structure, which offer apparent exceptions to the universality of this distinction.

3. Chemical Constitution. — The body of every living being is found to be composed of the essential elements, carbon, hydrogen, oxygen, and, probably, also, nitrogen, to which other simple substances may be superadded. No such uniformity can be predicated of the composition of· inorganic bodies.

4. Mode of increase. — The increment of inorganic bodies is effected by the addition of similar particles to their exterior, while that of living beings is due to the *assimilation* of nutrient matters received into the substance of their bodies. To such a mode of increase, the term *growth* is more properly applied.

The organic world includes two great groups of beings, *plants* and *animals*. These agree with one another in the possession of the above-mentioned characteristics, by which, as a whole, they differ from inorganic bodies. They agree, also, in their ultimate structural characters. They have, moreover, a similar origin, since both alike spring from *germs*, *i.e.* minute independent living molecules, for the production of which parent organisms are necessary. How then may they be distinguished from one another?

The larger animals, especially such as are either useful or dangerous to man, and with which, therefore, most persons are familiar, differ so much, in the adult condition, from the more conspicuous members of the vegetable kingdom, by reason of their powers of voluntary locomotion, as also by the anatomical feature of possessing a nervous system, that the present inquiry might seem, at first sight, unnecessary and even ridiculous. What resemblance is there, it might be asked, between a bird and the tree on which it perches, or a cow and the grass upon which it feeds ?

But the scientific naturalist is acquainted with numerous aquatic organisms, most (though not all) of these being of minute size, whose true position whether in the animal or vegetable kingdom has, of late years, afforded matter for abundant controversy. Many of these creatures, while presenting affinities to undoubted plants, are nevertheless capable of executing movements which have been frequently compared to those of animals. Besides, there are other living beings, fixed during the entire period of their lives, whose animal nature is not likely to be called in question. Further, several animal forms, universally recognised by naturalists as such, exhibit no traces of a nervous system.

The presence or absence of locomotive power, and of a nervous system, will, therefore, in many cases, be insufficient tests whereby to distinguish plants from animals. And the same must be said of all apparently more valid distinctions, drawn from chemical analysis of their respective tissues. There is, in short, no definable character, or combination of characters, common to all plants and foreign to all animals, or *vice versâ*.

Some persons, influenced by these considerations, have gone so far as to assert that there is no real line of demarcation between the animal and vegetable kingdoms, and that both merge insensibly into each other. Others have attempted to prove the existence of three distinct kinds of organised bodies, namely, plants, animals, and intermediate beings. Neither of these extreme views can be adopted. The popular opinion that there are two and only two great divisions of organic forms, distinct from one another, has been amply confirmed by the combined researches of our most able and trustworthy investigators, who believe that a line of separation between these two divisions does exist, though they may not be able precisely to define its limits. For it should be borne in mind, that the real difficulty now under consideration lies, not so much in our capability to determine whether any organism which may be offered for our inspection be a plant or an animal, since this, to any competent and unprejudiced observer, is seldom a matter of impossibility, but in framing such a definition as will embody our abstract conception of those essential and exclusive features, which separate the organic world into two distinct spheres of existence.

Nor should it be forgotten that those outward manifestations, which result from the presence of a locomotive apparatus and a material recipient of sentient impressions, though not exhibited by all animals, are by no means, on this account, less worthy of being considered as the most striking characteristics of animal life, of which, indeed, they are the peculiar *products*. In this point of view they were regarded by Aristotle[2], who has beautifully contrasted such active operations with the profound slumber in which the life of vegetables is plunged.

But of all the artificial distinctions which serve to separate plants from animals, none will be found more remarkable than those which are based, either on the nature of their respective nutrient materials, or the mode in which such materials are appropriated. The food of plants consists, for the most part, of the inorganic compounds, water, carbonic acid, and ammonia, together with minute quantities of a few mineral substances, usually to be found in most fertile soils. The Fungi, and other parasitic vegetables, are supposed to offer only apparent exceptions to the truth of this statement. Animals, on the other hand, require for their subsistence organised matter, which has been previously stored up in the bodies of other living beings. Again, plants imbibe their nutriment by means of absorbent organs situated on the exterior of their bodies, while the food of animals is first received into an internal digestive cavity, there to be subsequently elaborated. And even the greater number of those simple animal beings, in which no definite internal cavity can be perceived, would seem to have the power of forming one, as it were, extemporaneously, whenever its presence is called for to supply the wants of the organism.

Every animal, as a living being, possesses a definite form, which is itself the product of a number of definite parts or organs. In the higher animals, the number of these dissimilar parts attains its maximum. In others, no such complexity of structure is observable, and there are not wanting some animals, whose organisation is so exceedingly simple, that any differentiation of the body into separate parts can with difficulty be determined. There are also many animal forms of comparatively humble position, in which the entire fabric consists, not of a few distinct organs, each performing its special function, but of numerous parts similar to one another, and all fulfilling the same purpose. Such organisms are said to exhibit a tendency to a " vegetative (or irrelative) repetition of similar parts," [2] an expression which will be found convenient in practice, provided it be borne in mind that the " similar parts" are not distinct individuals.

The several organs of which animal forms are made up are all mutually related, or, in other words, certain leading peculiarities of structure are invariably found to co-exist with one another. This is termed the "correlation of forms." Some naturalists, not content with recognising the fact of such co-existence, have forsaken the true scientific method, and have sought to discover a causal relationship between the organs thus associated together. But morphology furnishes no answer to these futile inquiries.[4]

We compare the organs of different animals with a view to ascertain whether they agree in structure with one another. When such is the case, the corresponding organs are said to be "homologous." By some the word "morphology" is employed in a restricted sense, to signify the study of homologous organs. And it may here be mentioned that the term *Histology* has been applied to that branch of morphological science which is specially connected with the investigation of minute structure.

When two organs perform the same function, they are said to be "analogous" to one another. It is necessary to draw an important distinction between *analogy* and *homology*. For it is possible that two organs may correspond with one another in both structure and function, or in structure only and not in function, or again in function only and not in structure.

a

Under the title of the " Balancing of Organs " some morphologists have sought to establish a principle which may lead to the adoption of erroneous conclusions. This principle, rightly stated, is as follows : — The excessive development of one organ is often accompanied by a proportional deficiency in some other organ connected with it. But to this rule there are many exceptions, and in no case can it be proved that the atrophy or deficiency of one organ is the *result* of the extraordinary development of the other.

The several functions, or vital actions, of animals may be conveniently arranged under three groups, namely : --

1. Those which are subservient to the growth and maintenance of the organism — Functions of *Nutrition.*

2. Those which have reference to the continuance of the species — Functions of *Reproduction.*

3. Those which enable the animal to perform movements and become conscious of external impressions — Functions of *Relation.*

Of these, the Functions of Nutrition and Reproduction, being common to all organised beings, are sometimes designated " Functions of Organic or Vegetative Life," while the Functions of Relation are distinguished by the title of " Animal Functions."

The lowest form of animal life with which we

are acquainted has the power of maintaining its existence and increasing in size; it likewise executes perceptible movements, and gives rise to other beings similar to itself. So also is it with the most highly organised animal. What then is the nature of the physiological distinction between both?

In the simple animal being to which we have alluded it can scarcely be said that distinct organs exist, all parts of the body appearing to possess the power of performing, when called upon, any one of the necessary functions. In other animals, we recognise the presence of separate instruments for the discharge of each of the three great groups of functions above enumerated. In others, again, we find that one or more of these is resolvable into what may be termed " secondary functions," to each of which a special organ has been allotted. Finally, we meet with animals in which this " specialisation " of the functions and multiplication of dissimilar parts reaches its utmost extent. When such is the case, it is not difficult to show that the various vital actions are accomplished with a degree of completeness and efficiency not observable in those humble organisms whose position is at the base of the animal scale. All this is said to be in accordance with the principle of the physiological division of labour.

In the higher animals the nutritive processes are subdivided into functions of prehension, mastication, insalivation, deglutition, digestion, absorption, circulation, respiration, exhalation, excretion, secretion, and nutrition proper. It may further be noticed that these functions, being from their very nature necessary to the maintenance of the organism, are performed throughout the entire period of its existence.

It is not so with the Functions of Reproduction, the demand for which is often not manifested until the life of the individual has approached maturity, and even after that period it is not constant, but occasional. Moreover, the discharge of these functions, so far from being favourable to the maintenance of the organism, is, on the contrary, rather opposed to it, and it has even been observed that in some animals death always occurs shortly after the performance of the generative function.

The true generative act consists in the production of germs, and their subsequent contact with other bodies, termed 'spermatozoa.' The young germ is usually surrounded by a mass of nutrient matter (or yolk), and the whole together constitutes an 'ovum.' The contact of the ova and spermatozoa is termed 'fecundation.' Ova and spermatozoa may be generated in the same or in different individuals. Hence arises the distinction of sex; the power of producing ova being peculiar to the female, while the formation of spermatozoa devolves upon the male. It is well known that the two sexes are, in most cases, distinguished by various external peculiarities.

The independent being which results from the complete development of a fertilised ovum may subsequently multiply itself in various modes which have been grouped together under the common name of "asexual generation." These are all reducible to two processes, namely, 'fission,' or the division of the body into separate parts, and 'gemmation,' or the formation of buds. Gemmation may be either internal or external. When the products of the latter remain in connection with the parent organism, we are furnished with an illustration of the tendency to a vegetative repetition of similar parts; but should they separate from it in the form of seemingly independent beings, it then becomes difficult to distinguish between the results of fission and gemmation. Both of these processes are most easily observed among the lower animals.

Care must be taken not to confound the immediate offspring of the true generative act with the detached products of fission and gemmation. The former alone are properly denominated "individuals." The latter may be known by the name of "zoöids." Those who apply the term individual to these last are guilty of employing it in two distinct senses, for among the higher animals the apparent individual is always "equal to the total result of the development of a single ovum." [5]

It often happens that the zoöids resulting from fission or gemmation are very dissimilar in outward appearance to the organisms by which they were produced, while they possess the power of giving rise, by a true generative process, to beings exactly resembling the latter. In order to explain these phenomena, certain naturalists, ignorant of the distinction between "zoöid development" and sexual generation, devised the ingenious theory of "alternation of generations." But, from what has been said, it must appear that, in the instances referred to, there is not an alternation of two (or more) distinct generative acts, but rather an alternation of true generation with either gemmation or fission.

The functions of Relation may be divided into those of the muscular apparatus and those of the nervous system.

Were it possible for us to become acquainted with the structure and functions of any organism, our knowledge of its nature would still be imperfect so long as · we remained ignorant of its life history. Hence the necessity of the study of *Development*, which investigates the primitive characters of living beings, and the changes which they undergo in passing from the embryonic to the adult condition. Morphology, it may be said, teaches us what an animal *is*, Physiology what it *does*, Development what it *was*, and how from what it was it came to be what it is.

The study of development is, however, not merely desirable in itself; it is also absolutely requisite in the determination of homologies. Organs are usually said to be homologous when they correspond with one another in structure, and are connected with similar parts of their respective fabrics. But it would appear that these tests are sometimes fallacious, and, in the case of adult organisms, their application often becomes impossible. It is therefore necessary to compare the organs of different animals in their simplest condition, and to trace the several stages through which they pass, before it can be said that they agree with one another. And the same rule may be extended to the entire animals of which such organs form part.

A knowledge of development alone is capable of furnishing a solution to the inquiry, How far may unity of organisation be predicated of all animals? The answer is, in their primitive condition only, since the study of Morphology clearly shows the existence of distinct plans of structure among adult animals. All these start, as it were, from the same point, namely, the condition of the germ, and from this they rapidly diverge, each successive step in their development tending to separate them farther from one another. To the researches of the great Von Baer we are indebted for the enunciation of this important principle.[c]

Since the number of animal beings is exceedingly great, it seems needless to insist upon the necessity of arranging them into groups, so that they may be readily compared with one another But it must not be inferred that it is the sole or even the chief end of classification, so to facilitate reference that the relative position of any animal may be at once determined by means of easily recognisable external characters. Systems which propose to effect this object alone are termed *artificial*, and of such systems there may be several. True classification is contradistinguished by the term *natural*, since it may be defined as *the right appreciation of the mutual relations of animals, as dependent upon those characters and capacities which they have received from their Creator.* And as there is but one Author of Nature, so also there can be but one true interpretation of that Author's plan, though from insufficient knowledge and other causes, the various attempts to frame a natural classification which have hitherto been proposed, all differ more or less from one another in matters of detail.

We have already seen that animals may differ from one another in the varying complexity of their organisation. Differences of this kind, which are usually obvious, were supposed, by the

earlier naturalists, to furnish sufficient characters
whereby to distinguish the primary divisions of
the animal world.   It was afterwards ascertained
that these tests, however suitable they might at
first sight appear, were applicable only within certain limits.   For it is easy to select two animals,
in all essential features strikingly dissimilar,
though upon examination it will be found impossible to decide whether the organisation of one be
superior, as a whole, to that of the other.   Hence,
all arrangements which exhibit the animal kingdom as a continuous series, leading step by step
from the humblest of all animal forms to those in
which the specialisation of functions is most strongly
marked, are evidently unnatural.[7]   For as there
are two distinct points of view from which all
animals may be considered, so also one animal
may differ from another either as to the greater
or less complexity of its structure, or the general
plan upon which its structure has been framed.
Every animal, as Huxley has well observed, may
be regarded as the resultant of two tendencies, the
one physiological, the other morphological.[8]

By applying a process of generalisation to the
numerous facts which the study of morphology
has disclosed, we are led to the conclusion that
five ultimate plans of structure may be traced
among animal forms.   And accordingly the entire
animal kingdom may be divided into the same
number of primary groups, technically known

under the names of sub-kingdoms, branches, or departments, namely, —

VERTEBRATA.

MOLLUSCA.   ANNULOSA.

CŒLENTERATA.

PROTOZOA.

Sub-kingdoms are divided into classes, classes into orders, orders into families, families into genera, and genera into species.   It is usual to state that, "the species is a living form represented by individual beings, which reappears in the product of generation with certain invariable characters, and is constantly reproduced by the generative act of similar individuals."[9]   But it cannot be said that this definition is altogether unimpeachable.

It sometimes happens that between different individuals, known to belong to the same species, certain distinctive peculiarities are observable. When such peculiarities are strongly marked, the individuals which possess them are denominated *varieties*.   Permanent varieties, *i. e.* those which always produce offspring similar to themselves, are distinguished by the name of *races*.

The question how far individuals belonging to the same species may vary is intimately connected with that department of Zoölogy which treats of the Distribution of animal beings. For if it can be shown that animals are capable of becoming modified to an indefinite extent by the physical conditions under which they are placed, the following conclusions are inevitable:

1. That many of the apparently dissimilar animal forms found in different regions of the globe, are to be viewed as varieties of the same species, the differences between them being due to corresponding variations in the external agencies to which each has respectively been subjected.

2. That one species may pass into another, or, in other words, that species have no existence.

But since little positive evidence can be urged in favour of these conclusions, it seems desirable, for the present at least, to reject them as unsatisfactory, "for it is more probable that species should have been created with a certain degree of variability, than that mutability should be a part of the scheme of nature." It cannot, however, be denied that the tendency of several species to form varieties, is much greater than many naturalists are accustomed to admit.[10]

In considering the subject of distribution, it is necessary, as far as possible, to separate the facts of the science from the various theories which have been devised to explain them. The former, if rightly observed, may be accepted, since they exist in nature. The latter must be received with caution, since they are, for the most part, pure hypotheses.

Numerous observations show that some animals are very widely distributed, while others are restricted within narrow limits. Again, some districts contain a fauna (*i. e.* animal population) peculiar, or nearly so, to themselves; whilst others are peopled almost exclusively with derived species.

To account for these, and numerous other facts of a similar kind, it has been assumed that all the individuals of each species proceeded from one originally created pair; or, in the case of bisexual organisms, from a single parent. Each species must, therefore, have been at first confined within a very limited area; but being endowed with a power of diffusing itself, its descendants, after the lapse of time, became dispersed to a greater or less extent.[11]

There are, however, various causes which would tend to keep in check the migration of animals. Among these, an inability to exist outside a certain range of temperature is not the least important. For it has been proved that contiguous areas, with different climates, are inhabited by different species of animals. On the other hand, the effect of climate in determining the distribution of organised beings has been, in many instances, exaggerated. Other natural barriers, even more powerful, interpose to prevent the too wide-spread diffusion of both plants and animals.

The several facts which may be deduced from observation of the distribution of animals in Space, fall under the three following categories :—

1. The relations of animals to the elements in which they live.

2. Their lateral (geographical) distribution.

3. Their vertical (bathymetrical) distribution.

The distribution of animals in Time forms a distinct subject of inquiry, the consideration of which can only be entered on with profit by those who possess some acquaintance with the science of physical geology. It will, therefore, be sufficient here to state the following generalisations :—

Every species has a definite distribution in Time.

Each of the great geological epochs contained an assemblage of forms, different from one another, and the present.

In the older geological formations, there existed representatives of each of the five great divisions of the animal kingdom.

The animal remains found in these ancient formations, though referrible to the same classes, belonged, in many cases, to orders, families, genera, and species, different from those now living. In rocks of more recent date, the orders and families correspond to those at present existing, though the genera and species still remain dissimilar. Gradually, even these approximate; first the genera, and, finally, the species becoming identical with those of the present day.

NOTES.

1. In the 'Principles of Psychology,' by HERBERT SPENCER, various definitions of Life are discussed.

2. ARISTOTLE — Περι Ζωων Γενεσεως.

3. OWEN — 'Lectures on the Comparative Anatomy and Physiology of the Invertebrate Animals.'

4. See HUXLEY — 'On the Method of Palæontology,' (in Annals of Natural History, 1856.)

5. HUXLEY — 'Report upon the Researches of Professor Müller into the Anatomy and Development of the Echinoderms,' (in Annals of Natural History, 1851.)

6. VON BAER — 'Ueber Entwickelungs-geschichte der Thiere.' See also CARPENTER — 'Principles of Comparative Physiology.'

7. CUVIER, in a Paper read before the French Academy, first clearly announced the existence of distinct plans of structure in the Animal Kingdom. See his 'Règne Animal,' 2me edition.

8. HUXLEY — 'Lectures on General Natural History,' published in the Medical Times and Gazette.

9. J. MÜLLER — 'Handbuch der Physiologie des Menschen.'

10. J. D. HOOKER and T. THOMPSON — 'Introductory Essay to the Flora Indica.'

11. See LYELL — 'Principles of Geology;' and FORBES — 'On the Connection between the Distribution of the existing Fauna and Flora of the British Isles, and the Geological Changes which have affected their Area,' &c. (in the Memoirs of the Geological Survey of Great Britain, 1846.)

THE

SUB-KINGDOM

PROTOZOA.

PROTOZOA.

CHAPTER I.

PROTOZOA

1. General characters. — The sub-kingdom *Protozoa* includes a number of animal beings of simple organisation, many of which have, until recently, been associated with the lower members of the vegetable kingdom. Hence no good general definition can be given of this sub-kingdom, the several forms which it includes being distinguished from those which are placed in the four remaining zoological departments by chiefly negative characters. In none of the *Protozoa* do we find a nervous system or organs of sense, and, in many of these animals, the existence of a distinct alimentary apparatus has yet to be ascertained.

In the substance of the bodies of most *Protozoa* a minute solid particle known as the 'nucleus' is found to occur; and, in addition to this, the presence of certain clear spaces termed 'contractile vesicles' may, in some species, be traced.

B

In a large number of· the *Protozo ι* tɪue sexual reproduction has not yet been proⱱɛd to take place.

In habit the *Protozoa* are almost exclusively aquatic. Some attain to an appreciable, and even (in the case of the Sponges) considerable, size; but by far the greater number are minute, and hence, notwithstanding their abundance, the ignorance which still prevails as to their real nature.

2. **Classification.** — The following animal groups are included in this sub-kingdom, viz. · —

> 1. *Rhizopoda,*
> 2. *Polycystina,*
> 3. *Spongidæ,*
> 4. *Thalassicollidæ,*
> 5. *Gregarinidæ,*
> 6. *Infusoria.*

The presence of a mouth is characteristic of the *Infusoria,* and hence the remaining *Protozoa* are sometimes designated by the collective appellation of ' *Astomata.* '

CHAPTER II.

RHIZOPODA.

1. **Type of the group: Amœba.** — In order to understand the true nature of the *Rhizopoda* it will be necessary, in the first place, to become acquainted with those characters which are furnished by the examination of some typical form. The most easily procured of all Rhizopods is, perhaps, the *Amœba*, a minute animal not uncommon in most ponds or infusions (*fig.* 1).

When first placed under the microscrope the *Amœba* presents the appearance of a globular mass of semitransparent jelly, destitute of any apparent organisation. This seemingly helpless being soon, however, commences to show signs of life by pushing out in various directions portions of the jellylike substance of which its body is composed. By expanding one of these prolongations, and then drawing after it (or rather *into* it) the remainder of its body, the *Amœba* slowly advances, in a somewhat irregular manner. The gelatinous processes thus protruded have received the name of 'pseudopodia,' from their subservience to the function of locomotion. But this is not the only purpose which they serve. Should the *Amœba*, in its progress through the water, come in contact with any

B 2

foreign substance of small size, the latter is tena-
ciously grasped by the pseudopodia, which coalesce
around it, and thus the morsel soon becomes en-

Fig. 1.

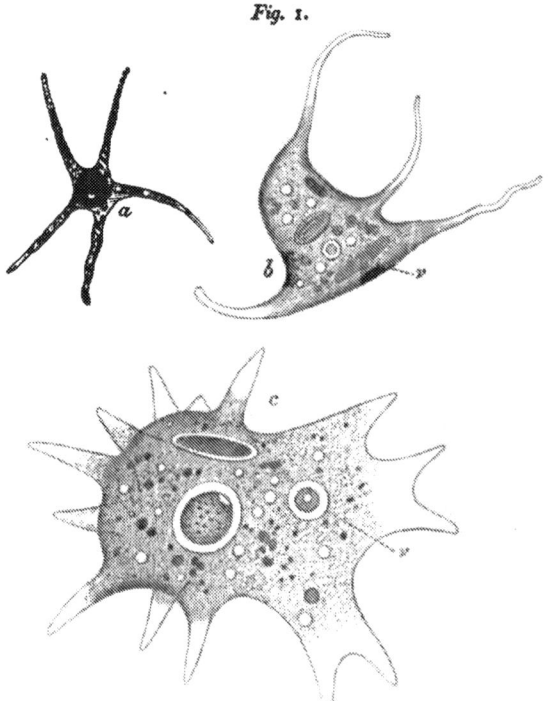

AMŒBA RADIOSA : — *a*, young *Amœba*, with five pseudopodia
protruded ; *b*, older specimen ; *c*, peculiar variety of do. ; *ν*,
the nucleus.

closed in the interior of the body.   There is no
true oral orifice, and the mode in which deglu-

tition is performed by the *Amœba* may not inaptly be illustrated by forcing a stone into the interior of a lump of clay or similar plastic material. The power of selection possessed by the *Amœba* would seem to be but slight, either as to the quantity or quality of its food. Inorganic particles, such as sand, are frequently ingested along with its more proper aliment. Sometimes the body of the *Amœba* appears as a mere transparent film investing the substance swallowed, and it occasionally happens that it becomes impaled on the sharp point of some projecting object. The indigestible remains of the food are finally pushed out through some part of the gelatinous body.

In the interior of the bodies of most *Amœbæ* a central solid particle or 'nucleus' (ν) may be observed, and, at certain times, one or more clear spaces or 'vesicles' may also be noticed. These contractile spaces are not permanent, but are seen to appear and disappear suddenly at more or less regular intervals. The colourless fluid, which they contain when dilated, would seem to be furnished during the process of digestion.

Physiologically, the *Amœba* may be regarded as the lowest of all animal forms, destitute of distinct organs, any part of its gelatinous body being capable of performing the functions of locomotion, digestion, &c., for the discharge of each of which a special, and often highly complicated, apparatus is set apart in the case of many of the higher animals. But, notwithstanding this simplicity of structure, several naturalists deem themselves justified in regarding the more permanent varieties of *Amœba* as so many distinct species; several of which have been described and figured by Auerbach.

In the body of one of these (*A. bilimbosa*), the existence of starch granules has been detected by the same observer.

2. **Nature of Rhizopoda.** — The structure of the remaining Rhizopods differs in no essential respect from that of *Amœba*. In all, the body is composed of the same simple gelatinous substance or 'sarcode,' as it has been termed by Dujardin, and in all, locomotion is performed by means of pseudopodia. From this circumstance, the group derives its name.

3. **Rhizopoda allied to Amœba.** — The so-called "sun animalcule" (*Actinophrys*), by some placed among the *Infusoria*, may be regarded as closely allied to *Amœba*. The form of its body (*fig.* 2, *a*) is that of a depressed sphere, furnished with a number of filiform pseudopodia radiating

Fig. 2.

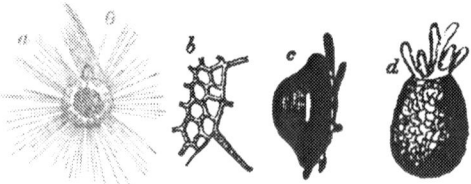

Various forms of RHIZOPODA : —*a*, *Actinophrys sol* in the act of feeding; at *θ* is shown a captured Infusorium which has just entered the substance of the body ; *b*, portion of the same, magnified 450 diameters ; *c*, *Arcella acuminata*; *d*, *Difflugia proteiformis*.

in all directions. These pseudopodia are usually somewhat longer than the diameter of the body, and are far less mutable than the same parts in *Amœba*. The body of *Actinophrys*, when magnified (*fig.* 2, *b*), is seen to be composed of a simple homogeneous sarcode substance, filled with granules and ' vacuoles,' in the midst of which a true ' contractile vesicle' may, in most cases, be readily perceived. The mode in which this Rhizopod takes food is peculiar, and has been carefully observed by Kölliker. Should a small Crustacean, Rotifer, or any other of the minute active animals upon which the *Actinophrys* is accustomed to feed, come in contact with one of the radiating filaments, it soon adheres to the latter, which slowly shortens until it approaches the surface of the body, the filaments in its neighbourhood bending around it, so that the prey becomes surrounded on all sides. The pseudopodia then gradually diminish in length, until that by which the prey was first seized altogether disappears. At this spot a depression begins to be formed, in which the captured animal is lodged (*fig.* 2, *a, θ*). This depression becomes deeper and deeper, the pseudopodia around it again elongate, and finally its outer edges coalesce, so that the prey becomes enclosed in a cavity. Here it remains until digested, after which the cavity contracts, and finally disappears. But should any indigestible particles remain, these are expelled by renewed contractions of the sarcode body, usually in the same direction by which they were originally taken in.

In both of the Rhizopods already noticed the body is completely naked. In some *Amœbæ*, indeed, its outer portion would seem to possess a certain degree of consistence, so as to serve as an envelope for the protection of the softer sarcode within. But in *Difflugia* we find it invested with a membranous 'carapace' or 'lorica,' of an oblong or oval figure, from the terminal aperture of which the pseudopodia are protruded (*fig.* 2, *d*). In *Arcella* the carapace assumes a discoid or hemispherical form (*fig.* 2, *c*), with the single narrow orifice placed on its flat surface. In both of these Rhizopods the surface of the carapace often exhibits tubercles or depressions, or has particles of sand, &c., imbedded in its substance; and in *Arcella* the margin is frequently provided with long spinous prolongations. The curious *Pamphagus*, described by Bailey, would seem to form a connecting link between these Rhizopods and *Amœba*. Like the latter, it is destitute of a carapace, but it agrees with *Arcella* and *Difflugia* in having the pseudopodia protrusible from one extremity only of the body. It undergoes the most extraordinary mutations of form, which are chiefly the result of its habit of swallowing almost every substance with which it comes in contact. Hence the appropriate name (*P. mutabilis*) conferred on this Rhizopod by its late discoverer.

4. **Classification of Rhizopoda.**—The Rhizopoda may be arranged under two sections, *Amœbea* and *Foraminifera*. The first of these may be again subdivided into two minor groups: 1. *Amœbina*, including those Rhizopods which have the body naked, viz. *Amœba*, *Actinophrys*, and *Pamphagus*; and 2. *Arcellina*, which contains *Difflugia* and *Arcella*. All these Rhizopods

were formerly placed among the *Infusoria*. They chiefly inhabit fresh water.

5. **Foraminifera**. — The *Foraminifera* differ from the *Amœbea* in being usually invested with a calcareous covering or 'shell,' which is sometimes simple, but more frequently consists of an aggregation of separate chambers or 'loculi' communicating with one another by means of minute apertures. In accordance with this character, the name *Foraminifera* has been given to the group. The appearance presented by these shells (*figs.* 3, and 4), both as regards outward configuration and internal arrangement, is often exceedingly complicated; and, in many cases, the same species presents itself to our notice under a wonderful diversity of forms. Accordingly, those naturalists by whom the *Foraminifera* were first studied, misled by external characters, assigned these animals a position far higher than that to which their internal structure entitled them. Their true nature was first explained by Dujardin, who showed that the animals inhabiting these calcareous shells differed in no essential respect from *Amœba* or *Arcella*, and that, like these forms, their bodies were composed of a homogeneous sarcode substance (*fig.* 3, *g'*). In some *Foraminifera*, this sarcode body is found to assume a bright red colour. The pseudopodia of these animals are usually longer and more slender than those of the *Amœbea*.

6. **Classification of Foraminifera**. — By D'Orbigny the *Foraminifera* have been divided into six "orders," viz. : —

1. *Monostega.* — Body consisting of a single segment: shell of one chamber.
2. *Stichostega.* — Body composed of segments disposed in a single line: shell consisting of a
   linear series of chambers.
3. *Helicostega.* — Body consisting of a spiral series
   of segments: shell made up of a number of
   convolutions.
4. *Entomostega.* — Body consisting of alternate
   segments spirally arranged: shell chambers
   disposed on two alternating axes forming a
   spiral.
5. *Enallostega.* — Body composed of alternate
   segments not forming a spiral: chambers arranged on two or three axes which do not
   form a spiral.
6. *Agathistega.* — Body consisting of segments
   wound round an axis: chambers arranged in
   a similar manner, each investing half the
   entire circumference.

All these orders, with the exception of the first,
are sometimes designated by the collective appellation of ' *Polythalamia.* '

A somewhat different arrangement has been
adopted by Schultze, who divides the *Polythalamia* into three sections, viz. : —

1. *Helicoidea,* including those forms in which
   the several chambers of the shell are arranged in a convolute series :
2. *Rhabdoidea,* in which they are placed in a
   direct line : and,
3. *Soroidea,* where they are disposed in an irregular manner. (*Vide* Table, p. 11.)

TABLE

SHOWING SCHULTZE'S ARRANGEMENT OF THE

RHIZOPODA.

A NUDA.

(Contains the genus AMŒBA.)

B. TESTACEA.

(Includes FORAMINIFERA and ARCELLINA.)

1. Monothalamia.

(= MONOSTEGA, D'Orbigny + ARCELLINA).

2. Polythalamia.

a. HELICOIDEA = $\begin{cases} \text{HELICOSTEGA, D'Orb.} \\ + \\ \text{ENTOMOSTEGA, D'Orb.} \\ + \\ \text{ENALLOSTEGA, D'Orb.} \\ + \\ \text{AGATHISTEGA, D'Orb.} \end{cases}$

b. RHABDOIDEA = (STICHOSTEGA, D'Orb.).

c. SOROIDEA. (Contains the genus ACERVULINA, Sch.)

All these arrangements may, however, be
regarded as premature, pending the result of
further investigations into the internal structure
of the shell, a more extended acquaintance with
which must form a necessary prelude to the
proper classification of the *Foraminifera*. Since,
moreover, we are unacquainted with the entire
life-history of any one of these animals, it is
evident that the time has not yet arrived for pro-
posing such an arrangement.

The truth of these observations will further appear when we consider that in the *Foraminifera*,
more perhaps than in any other group of animal
forms, is the same species liable to be influenced
by age, by the different circumstances in which it
is placed, or by both of these causes combined.
To assign the limit to which these variations may
extend is, in many cases, at present impossible.
For it has been fully proved, in more than one
well ascertained instance, that two or more varieties
of the same species obtained from distant localities,
or from the same locality, but at different stages
of growth, may present such dissimilarity of outward aspect as to require, for the determination of
their specific identity, the examination of many
hundred individual specimens, each gradually
passing into the other. Hence it is easy to con-
ceive how, by following too closely the arrangement of D'Orbigny, different varieties of the same
species have been placed in separate orders; the
principle on which his system has been founded,
namely, the direction of growth of the shell,
being obviously insufficient for the purposes of
classification.

Fig. 3.

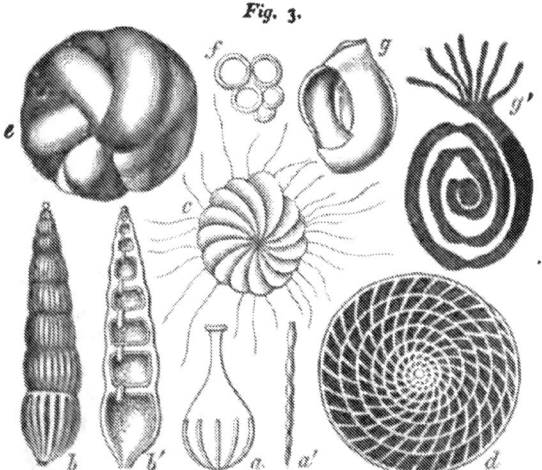

Various forms of FORAMINIFERA :— *a, Lagena striata ; a'
Nodosaria rugosa ; b, Marginulina (= Cristellaria) raphanus ;
b', longitudinal section of shell of do. ; c, Polystomella crispa,
with its pseudopodia protruded ; d, Nummulites lenticularis,
shown in horizontal section ; e, Cassidulina lævigata ; f, Textularia globulosa; g, Miliolina seminulum; g', animal of Miliolina
removed from its shell.*

7. **Unilocular Foraminifera.** — The Unilocular *Foraminifera* may be said to constitute an
intermediate group between the *Polythalamia* and
Arcellina; the form denominated *Gromia,* for
example, scarcely differing from *Difflugia* or *Arcella,* save in the greater length and tenacity of its
pseudopodia. A better example of these Rhizopods is furnished by *Lagena,* which may be sufficiently characterised by the beautiful flask-like
form of its shell (*fig.* 3, *a*), the external surface of

which frequently assumes a fluted appearance, caused by the presence of numerous longitudinal striæ. In addition to the outlet at the mouth of the shell the entire surface of the latter is perforated by a number of exceedingly minute apertures, through which the pseudopodia are protrusible. *Entosolenia* may be compared to *Lagena* with the tubular neck inserted into the hollow interior of the shell.

8. **Polythalamia**. — Among the *Polythalamia* the modifications in external configuration assumed by the shell would seem to be almost without limit. In *Nodosaria* (*fig.* 3, *a'*) it presents the aspect of a cylindrical beaded rod, which in *Lingulina* becomes compressed, and in *Dentalina* more or less curved, whilst in *Frondicularia* the peculiar sagittate form of the chambers will be found a distinctive test.

The term 'nautiloid' has been applied to a large group of multilocular Rhizopods, the shells of which present externally a remarkable resemblance to those of a well known group of Molluscous animals, including the Pearly Nautilus and its numerous extinct allies. It was this similarity of outward form which led the earlier naturalists to refer the *Foraminifera* to the class of Cephalopoda; a view of their nature which received the sanction of Cuvier and D'Orbigny, and continued to be generally adopted until the year 1835, when its incorrectness was fully demonstrated by Dujardin, who was the first to point out the simple nature of the animal body which occupied the interior of these many-chambered shells. These nautiloid forms constitute an extensive section of the order *Helicostega* of D'Orbigny. It has since, however, been shown that many Foraminiferous shells which commence their growth upon the spiral plan, e. g. *Cristellaria,* ultimately assume a straight form, so as to resemble *Nodosaria* (*fig.* 3, *b, b'*). Examples of nautiloid Rhizopods may be found in *Polystomella* (*fig.* 3, *c*), and in the well-known fossil *Nummulites* (*fig.* 3, *d*).

In *Cassidulina* (*fig.* 3, *e*) and its allies, each of the chambers of which the spiral shell consists is furnished with two surfaces of unequal size, which are alternately presented to opposite sides of the shell. Other modifications of the Polythalamous structure are presented by *Textularia* (*fig.* 3, *f*), and *Miliolina* (*fig.* 3, *g*), the nature of which will best be understood when we come to consider the mode of growth of the shell.

9. Structure of the Shell in Foraminifera.
— The structure of the shell has been ably investigated by Drs. Carpenter, Williamson, and others, whose combined researches have proved that its many complex forms all result from continuous processes of gemmation, and that the several varieties of these are dependent on corresponding variations in the plan upon which this gemmation is conducted. For all the multilocular Rhizopods consist at first of but a single chamber. Should the latter put forth another chamber similar to itself, and in a direct line with the axis of its body, this process, repeated several times, would give rise to such a form as *Nodosaria,* in which the original orifice of the first chamber serves as an aperture communicating between it and the

second, so that the several portions of the sarcode
body contained in the entire series of chambers
are all united by means of connecting bands
or 'stolons,' of the same substance (*fig.* 3, *b'*). If
the successive chambers gradually increase in
size, a conical shell will be produced. If, again,
each of the newly formed chambers, instead of
being developed in the axis of its predecessor, be
turned slightly to one side of the latter, the whole
series will assume a curved figure, and this may be
carried to such an extent as to confer on the entire
shell a spiral or convolute form. If the several
convolutions of one of these spiral forms all lie in
the same horizontal plane, as in *Polystomella* or
Nummulites (*fig.* 3, *c* and *d*), the shell is said to
be 'equilateral.' But if the successive chambers be
developed on one side of the plane of the first
chamber, so that the spiral passes obliquely round
an axis, the shell assumes a more or less pyra-
midal form, and is termed 'trochoid' or 'inequi-
lateral.' These latter terms may also be applied to
such shells as *Textularia* (*fig.* 3, *f*), which apparently consist of two or more oblique longitudinal
rows of chambers, but in reality differ only from
the true spiral forms in the smaller number of
chambers which occur in each of the convolutions.

A different mode of growth prevails among the
Miliolinæ. These are usually somewhat oblong in
figure, each of the newly formed chambers being
equal in length to the entire shell, so that, as
growth proceeds, the terminal orifice is alternately
transferred from one end of the shell to the other.
Hence, in these shells, the addition of successive
segments has been compared to the winding of the
thread round a ball of worsted (*fig.* 3, *g*).

In addition to the terminal orifice, which we have hitherto regarded as the sole growing point of the shell, many *Foraminifera* have the external surface of the latter perforated with numerous minute apertures, through which thread-like extensions of the sarcode body can be protruded (*fig.* 3, *c*); and it is not improbable that, by the coalescence of several of these, a layer is formed which may serve for the deposition of calcareous matter in the form of spines or other peculiarities of surface configuration. It would seem, however, that in *Faujasina*, *Operculina*, and certain other *Polythalamia*, these foramina are not to be regarded as simple apertures in the walls of the chambers, but rather as the orifices of a peculiar system of ' interseptal ' canals, which after ramifying between the walls of contiguous chambers proceed directly to the innermost portion of the shell, serving to bring those parts of the sarcode body which are contained in the latter into immediate communication with the exterior. In *Nummulites* and other fossil forms these canals have been observed to increase both in number and complexity of arrangement; for here, in addition to the regular series of chambers, there exists an ' interstitial skeleton ' for the nutriment of which this increased development of the ' canal system,' would appear to be required. Hence it has been said that these *Polythalamia* present us with the highest and most fully developed type of Foraminiferous structure.

A mode of growth distinct from any of the preceding has been observed by Dr. Carpenter to take place in another group of *Foraminifera*, of which *Orbitolites* may be regarded as the type.

c

If the circular flattened disk of one of these forms
(*fig.* 4, *a*) be submitted to microscopic examination, a series of rounded elevations disposed in
concentric annular bands round a central "nucleus" may be observed on its surface, whilst its
margin is seen to consist of an undulating succession of rounded projections alternating with depressions, each of the latter being provided with
a single orifice. On more careful examination,
we find that each of the rounded elevations constitutes the upper surface of a chamber or cell,
"which communicates by means of a lateral
passage with the cavity on either side of it in the
same ring; so that each circular zone of cells might
be described as a continuous annular passage,
dilated into cavities at intervals. On the other
hand, each zone communicates with the zones
that are internal and external to it, by means of
passages in a radiating direction; and it is curious
that these passages run, not from the cells of the
inner zone to those of the outer; but from the connecting passages of the former to the cells of the
latter; so that the cells of each zone *alternate* in
position with those of the zones that are internal
and external to it. The radial passages from the
outermost annulus make their way at once to
the margin, where they terminate, forming the
'pores' which (as already mentioned) are to be
seen on its exterior. The central nucleus, when
rendered sufficiently transparent (by previous pre-
paration), is found to consist of a central cell (ν),
usually somewhat pear-shaped, that communicates
by a narrow passage with a much larger circumambient cell (π), which nearly surrounds it, and
which sends off a variable number of radiating

passages towards the cells of the first zone, which forms a complete ring round the nucleus."

If the animal of *Orbitolites* be decalcified by

Fig. 4.

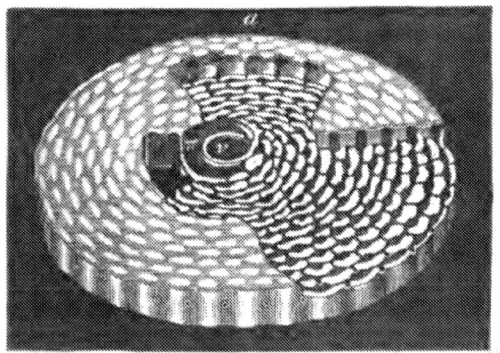
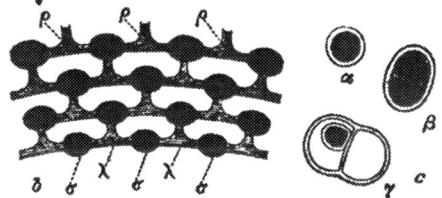

Structure of ORBITOLITES COMPLANATUS: — *a*, simple disk of *Orbitolites*, laid open to show its interior ; *v*, central cell; *x*, circumambient shell, surrounded by concentric zones of cells, connected with each other by annular and radiating passages ;— *b*, portions of sarcode body of the same, showing σ, σ, σ, segments of sarcode contained in the ovate cells ; λ, λ, their annular, and ρ, ρ, ρ, their radial stolons ;—*c*, peculiar reproductive (?) bodies ; *a*, gemmule, embedded in sarcode substance ; β, the same, undergoing fission ; γ, another gemmule, found in one of the superficial cells.

maceration in dilute acid, the above arrangement will be rendered still more evident (*fig. 4, b*).

For the contents of the ovate cells are seen to consist of segments of sarcode (σ, σ, σ), from which stolons are prolonged into the interior of both the radial and annular passages (ρ, ρ, ρ, and λ, λ). Each of the concentric zones of segments is, in all probability, produced by gemmation from the zone immediately within it, the segments of the innermost zone having been originally budded off by extensions of the sarcode body contained in the circumambient cell, which, again, in its turn, is connected by means of a narrow stolon with the pear-shaped mass of the same substance occupying the interior of the central cell. There can be also but little doubt that, in the living animal, the radial stolons of sarcode which proceed from the outermost annulus are enabled to send forth pseudopodia through the marginal pores, the latter being the only external apertures which the shell of the Orbitolite possesses; and analogy would suggest that these pseudopodia may not only serve for the prehension of food, but may also, by the coalescence of several round the margin of the shell, give rise to the deposition of successive layers of calcareous matter.

Such is the ordinary structure of Orbitolite. But the same form is sometimes met with under a much more complicated type, in which the thickness of the entire shell is considerably increased, and the marginal pores are seen to be arranged in several rows, placed one above another. Here the superficial cells, which in the simple type are either round or oval, become nearly rectilinear, having their long diameters placed at right angles to the centre of the disk. Each of the segments of sarcode contained in these oblong chambers communicates by means of a double footstalk with a pair of circular stolons, a concentric series of which lie beneath both the upper and lower surfaces of the shell. These two sets of stolons are connected with one another by means of linear bands of sarcode, enclosed in columnar chambers which run through the intermediate thickness of the disk. Each of these linear bands sends forth a double series of sarcode threads, which serve to bring it into connection with a pair of the columns belonging to the zone on its interior, those of the outermost zone having probably the power of protruding pseudopodia through the numerous rows of marginal apertures.

The *texture* of the shell is also deserving of notice. In *Gromia* and a few other forms it is somewhat membranous, whilst in *Proteonina* it is arenaceous. These, however, are exceptional instances, since in the greater number of *Foraminifera* the shell is eminently calcareous, presenting various degrees of consistence. In *Lagena* it is hyaline, but in *Miliolina* and its allies it becomes unusually opaque, so as nearly to resemble white porcelain. In newly formed segments, the shell is usually deficient in thickness.

10. **Technical Terms.** — For the better description of the multilocular Rhizopods certain technical terms have been proposed. Thus the several chambers of which the shell consists have received the name of *segments*, that from which all the others originate by a process of gemmation being known as the *primordial*, whilst that

which is last formed is termed the *ultimate* segment. Each of the segments, viewed externally,
is said to have two margins, the *anterior*, which is
nearest the ultimate segment, and the *posterior*,
which is nearest the primordial one. The parti-
tions which separate the contiguous segments
from one another are termed *septa*, each of which
is perforated by one or more *septal* apertures, and
in most cases indicated externally by a ridge or
depression, called the *septal line*. The superficial
area of each septum, corresponding with the entire breadth of that portion of the shell where it
occurs, has been designated the *septal plane*.

In the nautiloid forms the term *spiral suture*
is employed to denote the line by which each
convolution is separated from that on either side
of it. Here the entire shell is said to have two
lateral surfaces, and a *peripheral* margin. The
shape of the latter, which varies considerably in
different forms, determines also that of the septal
planes. Each of these last forms three angles,
the *peripheral* and the two *umbilical* angles, the
latter being so termed because " directed towards
the centre of each lateral surface occupied by the
primordial segment, where there is usually a depression or *umbilicus*." Each of the segments
also has three margins, an anterior, a posterior,
and a peripheral. It has likewise two angles, an
anterior umbilical and a posterior umbilical.

In the trochoid shells the surface on which the
primordial segment appears is termed the " posterior," while the opposite extremity is known as the
inferior, lateral surface.

Among the straight types, such as *Nodosaria*,
the term " *lateral aspect* " is applied to the shell,

when seen in its ordinary position, its *anterior* aspect being presented to our view when we look down from above on the septal plane of its ultimate segment. In *Lingulina* and other compressed forms, the sides of the shell, when viewed edgeways, are said to present their "*periphero-lateral*" aspect, the same term being also applied to the Nautiloid shells, when viewed in the direction of their peripheral margins.

11. **Distribution of Foraminifera in space.** — By far the greater number of *Foraminifera* are marine. They are found in most seas, preferring, however, those of tropical and southern climes, where an increase may be observed, not merely in the number and variety of the specimens, but likewise in the size which several of the latter attain. Many of the *Foraminifera* have been dredged from considerable depths, some in a a living state; and there is reason to believe that extensive deposits of their shells, associated with those of other minute organisms, are in process of formation on several parts of the existing sea bottom, more especially in the North Atlantic, the Eastern Mediterranean, and the Australian Seas.

Among the more widely distributed animals of the present group may be especially mentioned *Orbulina* and *Globigerina*, both of which forms may be regarded as almost cosmopolitan.

Specimens of *Foraminifera* may be obtained for examination from the shakings of dried Sponges, or even from the sand on most parts of the sea coast: but, should they be required for observation of the contained animal, they must be dredged for

this purpose from suitable localities, or picked,
with the aid of a lens, from the fronds of living
sea weeds, over the surface of which they may be
observed to crawl by means of their pseudopodia.

12. **Distribution of Foraminifera in time.**
— Remains of *Foraminifera* have been proved to
exist in most of the stratified rocks, from the
Silurian to the Tertiary inclusive; many of the
forms found in the older formations being nearly,
if not absolutely, identical with those which occur
in the seas of our own epoch. But the insufficient
and superficial manner in which the "genera" and
"species" of these animals have too frequently
been characterised, has considerably deducted from
the value of those facts from which conclusions
might otherwise be deduced with reference to their
distribution.

Among Paleozoic strata remains of these animals have been found to occur in both the Silurian
and Carboniferous series. The green grains which
lie scattered through the Lower Silurian sand-
stones of the neighbourhood of St. Petersburgh
have been shown by Ehrenberg to contain in their
interior siliceous casts of Foraminiferous shells,
some of which are referrible to such existing forms
as *Guttulina, Rotalia*, and *Textularia*. The two
last mentioned of these have been likewise detected in the Carboniferous limestone, certain beds
of which, found in Russia and the United States,
are composed, for the most part, of the shells of
Fusulina, a form which would seem to be exclusively confined to this deposit.

Among secondary rocks, *Foraminifera* prevail
in both the oolite and chalk, being, however, more

numerous in the latter, extensive beds of which are in many districts made up of little else than the shells of *Rotalia, Spirulina,* and *Textularia.*

But it is in the formations of the Tertiary period that this group may be said to have attained its greatest development. It is here we first meet with the widely distributed *Nummulites,* whose size, compared with that of any *Foraminifera* which have preceded them, must be considered as gigantic. They are chiefly characteristic of the Middle Eocene; and it has been proposed by some geologists to divide this formation into three sections, each being distinguished by a separate form of Nummulite. The extent to which some of these strata prevail has been thus indicated by Sir Charles Lyell.

" The Nummulitic formation, with its characteristic fossils, plays a far more conspicuous part than any other tertiary group in the solid framework of the earth's crust, whether in Europe, Asia, or Africa. It often attains a thickness of many thousand feet, and extends from the Alps to the Carpathians, and is in full force in the North of Africa, as, for example, in Algeria or Morocco. It has also been traced from Egypt, where it was largely quarried of old for the building of the Pyramids, into Asia Minor, and across Persia, by Bagdad, to the mouths of the Indus. It occurs not only in Cutch, but in the mountain ranges which separate Scinde from Persia, and which form the passes leading to Caboul; and it has been followed still farther eastward into India, as far as Eastern Bengal and the frontiers of China."

It has been shown by Dr. Carpenter that the Nummulitic limestone of some districts contains

the remains, not of *Nummulites* proper, but rather
of a form which, though resembling it closely in
external appearance, is in internal structure very
dissimilar. For this form he has proposed the
name of *Orbitoides*. The same observer has also
given it as his opinion, that between the existing
Nonionina and the true fossil *Nummulites* there
exists no important difference of structure.

13. **Size of Rhizopoda.** — All the *Amœbea*
are microscopic, being seldom known to exceed
·02 of an inch in diameter. The *Foraminifera* are
somewhat larger, the linear dimensions of the
recent British species (for example) varying from
·005 to ·050 of an inch. But among the tropical
and extinct forms of the group we meet with
many whose size is much more considerable;
Nummulites being frequently at least three inches
in circumference, while specimens of *Cyclocly-
peus* have been met with which have been found to
reach 2·25 inches in diameter.

14. **Development of Rhizopoda.** — Almost
nothing is known of the development of the *Rhizopoda*. *Difflugia* and *Actinophrys* have been
observed to undergo multiplication by fission (i. e.
the separation of the body into two parts), and the
last-mentioned form also propagates itself by a
peculiar method which presents some slight analogy to the " conjugating process" among the
lower Algæ. In the body of *Orbitolites* Dr. Carpenter has observed the sarcode to be " broken up
(as it were) into little spherules," and these he sup-
poses are probably " gemmules " destined for ex-
pulsion through the marginal pores. He has also

detected, imbedded in the sarcode, certain other bodies (*fig.* 4, *c*), which may be either "gemmules in a later stage or possibly true ova (?)." These exhibit various stages of binary division, and always present a deep red colour. But their exit, and subsequent development, have hitherto escaped observation.

———

CHAPTER III.

POLYCYSTINA.

1. Nature. — 2. Distribution.

1. **Nature**. — The name *Polycystina* was first given by Ehrenberg to a group of minute shell-bearing organisms, apparently allied to the *Foraminifera*. They are usually of smaller size than the latter, from which also they differ in the nature of their shelly investment, the composition of which is siliceous. These shells are remarkable for the great beauty and variety of their forms,

Fig. 5.

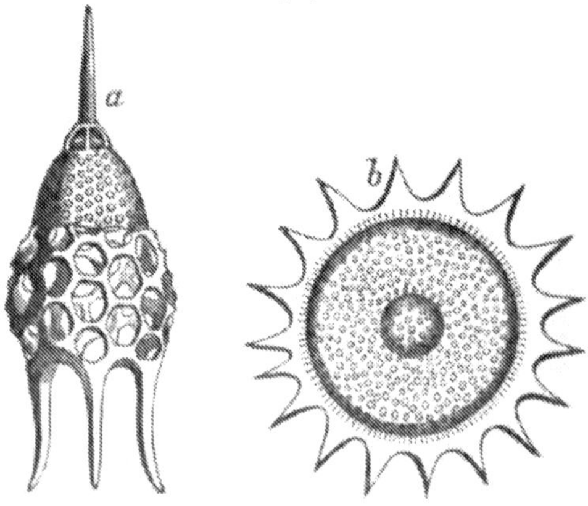

POLYCYSTINA : — a, *Podocyrtis Schomburgkii*; b, *Haliomma Humboldtii.*

and the peculiar appearance of the spine-like projections with which they are frequently fur-

nished (*fig. 5*). The contained animal consists
of an olive brown sarcode substance capable of
protruding pseudopodia through the numerous
foramina with which the shell is perforated. In
those forms which have been most carefully examined, the sarcode-body, which is divided into four
equal lobes, does not fill the entire cavity of the
shell, but would seem to be wholly confined to the
upper portion of the latter. Of the true nature of
these creatures, much has yet to be learned.

2. **Distribution.** — The *Polycystina* are very
widely distributed. Their shells, mingled with
those of *Foraminifera* and *Diatomaceæ*, have been
ascertained to form part of the extensive organic
deposit which is now being formed over a portion
of the bed of the North Atlantic. They have been
found also in the Mediterranean and various other
parts of the existing ocean. They appear, however, to have been even more numerous at former
periods, their remains having been already detected in both the secondary and tertiary formations. Nearly 300 apparently distinct forms of
these animals have been discovered by Ehrenberg,
in a tertiary deposit which occurs abundantly
throughout an extensive district of the island of
Barbadoes.

CHAPTER IV.

SPONGIDÆ.

1. **Animal nature.** — If the animal nature of the Rhizopoda be admitted, that of the Sponges can no longer be regarded as doubtful. For a Sponge consists of a soft gelatinous substance, supported by an internal framework or skeleton, the whole being usually strengthened by the addition of calcareous or siliceous 'spicula.' The soft gelatinous flesh is found, on examination, to be composed of an aggregation of amœbiform bodies, and must be considered as constituting the essential part of the animal, since in some Sponges the skeleton is altogether absent, whilst in others the mineral spicula are replaced by particles of sand.

In *Grantia* (one of the marine Sponges) the amœba-like particles are furnished with long filamentary appendages, which have received the name of 'cilia' (*fig. 6, e*). To these peculiar organs, which now for the first time make their appearance in the animal kingdom, we shall hereafter more fully allude (p. 66). Ciliated particles have likewise been noticed in the gelatinous substance of the fresh-water Sponges (*Spongilla*); but here they are not present at all times of the year, having been observed to disappear on the approach of winter, during which season the body

of *Spongilla* solely consists of amorphous non-
ciliated amœbiform bodies.   But it is right to
mention that the structure of these last is asserted by Lieberkühn to be not quite so simple
as some naturalists have supposed.

Fig. 6.

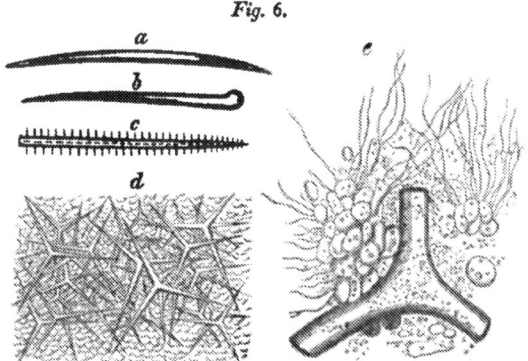

Structure of GRANTIA, &c.:—*a*, *b*, *c*, siliceous spicula of *Hali-
chondria*; *d*, portion of *Grantia compressa*, showing arrangement of triradiate (calcareous) spicula ; *e*, smaller portion of
the same (more highly magnified), showing ciliated amœbiform
particles.

2. **Form and Size**. —The various kinds of
Sponges present themselves to our notice under
every possible diversity of size and outward
configuration.   Some form flattened incrustations
investing the surfaces of rocks, shells, and various
submarine objects ; others occur as dense compact
masses, often of considerable dimensions ; others,
again, are erect, cup-shaped ; while not a few
assume the aspect of branching arborescent struc-

tures. In size, the Sponges far exceed all other
Protozoa; aggregate masses of these animals being
sometimes met with, chiefly on the shores of tropical seas, which cover surfaces of many yards in
extent.

3. **Skeleton.** — The skeleton or framework of
the Sponge, which is best seen in dried specimens,
is usually composed of a number of horny fibres,
anastomosing one with another in such a manner as
to form an irregular though intricate network. In
some sponges, e. g. *Grantia*, this fibrous network
is altogether wanting. In the Sponges of com-
merce it attains an unwonted degree of softness
and elasticity, which qualities, combined with the
comparative paucity of their spicula, give to these
substances their chief value in a commercial
point of view. In certain tropical Sponges, on the
other hand, it is found to be entirely made up of
siliceous particles; these, however, still presenting
that characteristic reticulated arrangement which
may be regarded as essentially distinguishing the
' fibre' from all the other structures which together
make up the body of the Sponge.

4. **Aquiferous System.** — With the porous
aspect of ordinary Sponges most persons are
familiar. On more careful examination it will be
seen that these pores are of two kinds: 1. the
larger pores, which are comparatively few in number and frequently elevated on slight prominences;
and 2. the smaller pores, which are much more
numerous, crowding the entire surface of the
Sponge so as to occupy the interspaces between
the larger apertures. The latter are properly de-

nominated 'oscula,' the smaller orifices being specially distinguished as the 'pores.'

On cutting open the Sponges, the oscula and pores are seen to be connected each with its proper system of 'canals.' What are termed the 'excurrent' canals proceed immediately from the oscula, and, after forming a somewhat complicated network within the outer layer of the Sponge, finally communicate with another system of 'incurrent' canals, which, in their turn, terminate in the 'pores.' Both of these sets of canals are produced by the peculiar arrangement of the horny fibres which compose the skeleton, and in the living animal are invested on all sides by a coating of the glairy gelatinous sarcode.

If a fragment of living Sponge be placed, in a watch-glass, on the stage of a microscope and examined with a low magnifying power, a curious spectacle will, under favourable circumstances, come into view. Currents will be seen to issue rapidly from the oscula, whilst at the same time water is being continually absorbed by the pores. In this manner a sort of circulation is maintained within the two systems of canals which connect the oscula and pores with one another. The currents are rendered more readily observable, by diffusing finely powdered indigo or carmine in the water containing the specimens under examination.

When the foregoing phenomena were first noticed (in 1827) by Dr. Grant, they excited much attention among naturalists, though for a long time afterwards the mechanism by which they were effected, remained altogether undiscovered. More recently the subject has been investigated

D

anew by Dr. Bowerbank, from whose observations, made, for the most part, on the common fresh-water Sponge, the following conclusions seem deducible, viz. : —

1. That the circulatory action is, in all probability, due to the presence of vibratile cilia.
2. That these cilia (if present) are situated, not around the oscula or pores, but rather within the larger excurrent canals which run immediately beneath what may be termed the "dermal membrane" of the Sponge.
3. That the circulatory action is, to a certain extent, periodical, continuing for a sufficient length of time to enable nutrient particles to be conveyed to all parts of the interior of the Sponge, after which it becomes languid for a while, to be again resumed, when its performance is called for to supply the necessities of the organism.

And further, it has been proved,

4. That the living animal possesses the power of opening and closing its oscula at pleasure;
5. That the several oscula may act more or less independently of one another ; and
6. That new oscula may be formed, if required, anywhere in the course of the larger excurrent canals.

It is obvious that the above currents may be employed, not merely in the conveyance of food, but likewise in the removal of effete matter. They contribute, moreover, to the general aëration of the entire animal, presenting us, it may be said,

with the first indication of a respiratory apparatus.
It would seem also that the nutrient matters conveyed by the currents to the interior of the canals
are there assimilated by the sarcode substance
lining the latter, much in the same way that particles of food are appropriated by the gelatinous
processes of *Actinophrys* or *Amœba.*

5. **Reparative powers.** — The reparative
powers which many Sponges possess are by no
means the least remarkable of their vital phenomena. If the substance of the Sponge sustain in-
jury by incision or otherwise, the wounded surfaces will be found, in the majority of instances,
after a short time, to have completely healed. It
has also been proved that separate fragments belonging to the same species of Sponge, if placed in
contact and allowed to remain undisturbed, will
often, within a few hours, unite together, so as to
form a single specimen; and it has been further
ascertained that the process of adhesion is in no
wise interrupted by suffering the water to drain
away from the specimens which are made the subject of experiment.

6. **Spicula.** — The spicula or mineral bodies,
which are found in the majority of Sponges, vary
considerably both in form and size (*figs.* 6 and 7).
They occur throughout all the various structures
of the animal, each of whose parts is stated by
Dr. Bowerbank to contain its appropriate forms
of these bodies; one kind of spicules being found
in the skeleton, another in the sarcode substance,
whilst others, which project beyond the surface of
the Sponge, are presumed to be of use in defending

their possessor from the attacks of other animals.
Those which occur in the sarcode are usually of
the kind which have been denominated 'stellate,'
many of them presenting a curious complexity of
structure. Other spicules, whose forms are no less
peculiar, are found in connection with the so-called
' gemmules' and similar reproductive bodies : thus
in *Spongilla*, each of the spicula by which the
" seed-like body " is surrounded presents the appearance of a pair of toothed wheels united together by an axle (*fig.* 8).

The composition of the spicula is, in most cases,
siliceous, but in *Grantia* and a few other forms
they are found to be composed of carbonate of
lime.

It is evident from the peculiarity and constancy
of the forms which spicula assume, and from the
total absence of anything which can be compared
to a crystalline structure, that they are to be regarded as true organic deposits, resulting, it would
seem, from the vital endowment of segments of
the sarcode body especially set apart for their secretion.

7. **Classification.** — We possess no good classification of the Sponges, the several " genera " and
" species " into which this group of animals is
usually divided having been far too insufficiently
examined to permit any arrangement of them
which has hitherto been proposed to be regarded
as aught else than temporary. We shall therefore
select as an example of this section of the *Protozoa* the form denominated *Tethya*, not that it is
to be regarded as its most typical representative,
but rather because its structure has been more

fully investigated than that of most other members of the group.

8. **Structure of Tethya.** — From the observations of Prof. Huxley it would appear that this Sponge consists essentially of three distinct structures, viz. : —

1. A central, whitish, spherical substance (*fig.* 7, *b*, λ); composed of a granular mass, associated with numerous cylindrical spicula.
2. A yellowish red intermediate portion (*fig.* 7, *b*, β); composed of a granular uniting substance in which ova and stellate spicula (*a*, κ) are embedded.
3. A deep red cortical substance (*b*, *a*); consisting of two zones, which merge insensibly into one another. Of these, the inner is composed of closely interwoven bundles of a fibrous tissue, and contains only a small number of stellate spicules, whilst the outer zone is dense, granular, " containing great numbers of crystalline spheres beset with short conical spikes."

The rod-like spicula which occur in the central substance are usually so arranged as to form an irregular network, becoming aggregated into bundles as they approach the intermediate substance. The several spicula contained in these bundles are at first nearly parallel to one another, but they gradually diverge as they radiate through the latter, terminating at length, in the cortical layer, beyond which a small number not unfrequently project. Numerous long solitary rods, in addition to the bundles, also radiate through the interme-

diate substance.   The longitudinal axis of each of
the rods is traversed by a very narrow canal.

To return to the intermediate substance.   Its
granular mass is found to be altogether made up
of small circular cells (a, ω), "and of spermatozoa in every stage of development from those
cells.   The cell throws out a long filament which
becomes the tail of the spermatozoon, and becoming
longer and pointed forms, itself, the head.   The
perfect spermatozoa have long, pointed, somewhat
triangular heads about $\frac{1}{3000}$ of an inch in diameter,
with truncated bases, from which a very long filiform tail proceeds."

" The ova (a, o) are of various sizes. The largest
are oval and about $\frac{1}{500}$ of an inch in long diameter.

Fig. 7.

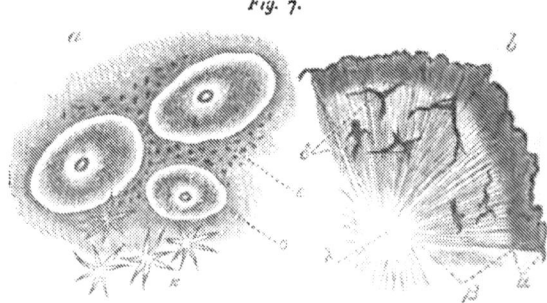

Structure of TETHYA :— a, portion of the intermediate substance of *Tethya* (magnified), showing o, ova embedded in sper-
matic mass (ω), together with stellate bodies (κ);—b, section of
Tethya (nat. size), showing λ, central portion, β, intermediate
substance, a, cortical layer, δ, canals.

They have a very distinct vitellary membrane,
which contains an opaque coarsely granular yolk."

In the centre of each, surrounded by a clear space may be noticed the 'germinal vesicle,' and within the latter a minute 'germinal spot' may sometimes be seen.

9. **Development**.—The development of the Sponges is effected,

    a. by ova and spermatozoa;

    b. by various other bodies, the true nature of which is not yet sufficiently determined.

a. True reproduction has hitherto been proved to take place in *Tethya* alone, although from analogy, there can be little doubt that it must

Fig. 8.

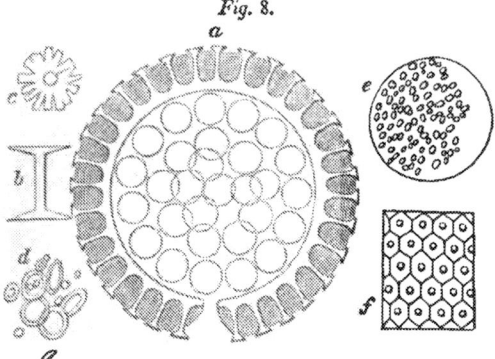

Structure of seed-like body of SPONGILLA:— *a*, one of the seed-like bodies of *Spongilla Meyeni*, shown in magnified section; *b*, one of its spicula seen in profile; *c*, the same, viewed endways; *d*, germs of cells of *a* (very much magnified); *e*, one of the cells of *a*, containing germs; *f*, portion of coriaceous membrane of *a*, showing hexagonal divisions and transparent centres.

also occur in most other forms of the group. In the fresh-water Sponges small moving corpuscles, similar to the spermatozoa of *Tethya* have been recently detected by Lieberkühn.

b. Carter has described certain "seed-like bodies" (*fig.* 8, *a*) which are found embedded in the gelatinous substance of *Spongilla*. Each of these consists of a round or ovoid coriaceous capsule, the surface of which when magnified, presents a hexagonally tessellated appearance (*f*), and is surrounded by a zone of the peculiar asteroid spicula (*b*, *c*) to which we have already referred (p. 36), these being embedded in a coating of gelatinous matter. Within the capsule are numerous, transparent, spherical "ovi-bearing cells" containing granules and germs in their interior (*d*, *e*), and surrounded by a cortical layer of peculiar nucleated cells. When arrived at maturity the contents of the seed-like body escape through the hilum or aperture with which it is provided, "under the form of a gelatinous mass, in which the ovi-bearing cells and their contents appear to be embedded entire." Next, spicula are developed and with them a delicate pellicle or "investing membrane" which would seem to be formed from the nucleated cells of the cortical layer. This becomes separated by an interval or "cavity" from the "parenchyma" or gelatinous substance enclosing the ovi-bearing cells. Apertures subsequently originate in the investing membrane, whilst at the same time a canal system is being formed in the parenchyma; and, finally, the ovi-bearing cells are developed into a number of stomachal or "ampullaceous" sacs, which open into the incurrent canals.

From the investigations of Lieberkühn it would appear that the propagation of *Spongilla* is sometimes effected by peculiar bodies to which the name of "swarm spores" has been given. These were oval in form; more pointed at one end than at the other and consisted of three distinct substances; viz. 1, an epithelial cellular envelope; 2, a structureless cortical layer; and 3, an interior spheroidal medullary portion. The latter is resolvable into an exterior mucoid layer, containing a variable number of "germ granules," embedded in an albuminous substance and associated with numerous minute siliceous spicula. The swarm spores were actively locomotive, swimming rapidly about by means of the cilia which were disposed in a regular manner over the entire surface of their bodies. After leading a somewhat restless existence for one or two days they sunk to the bottom of the vessel wherein they were confined, to which they soon after began to adhere. The greater number decayed; a few, however, were observed to expand into a delicate layer consisting of a gelatinous substance in which minute siliceous needles were embedded, and at length, on the 20th day, the characteristic Sponge structures made their appearance.

In addition to the germ-granules contained in the swarm spores, spherical aggregations of the same bodies, in a free condition, were not unfrequently met with. They were found in all parts of *Spongilla*, being especially abundant at the base or attached portion of the mass.

With regard to the nature of the above swarm spores, and the relation which exists between them and the seed-like bodies, much has yet to be learned. Carter asserts that they are merely ciliated forms of the latter, a statement which, however

probable, must for the present be considered as
unproven.

In the interior of the canals of some marine
Sponges minute bud-like extensions of the sarcode
substance may readily be observed at certain sea-
sons of the year, and these, which are provided
with cilia, detach themselves from the body of the
parent, and probably, at length becoming fixed,
give rise to new Sponge formations. But it may
be questioned whether these bodies have not been,
in many cases, confounded with true ciliated
swarm spores, similar to those which are found in
Spongilla.

10. **Distribution.** — The distribution of the
Sponges may be compared, in many respects, to
that of the *Foraminifera.* Like them they are
almost exclusively marine, are found in most
climates, but occur most abundantly, are more
varied in form, and luxuriant in growth, on the
shores of the warmer regions of the globe. Like
them also they have been found in most of the
geological epochs from the Silurian period to the
present. The Sponges of the chalk have more
especially attracted attention, the well known flint
nodules of that formation, in many cases, owing
their peculiar form to the presence of the extinct
remains of these animals. Several fossil Spongidæ
have been figured and described of which *Palæo-
spongia* is said to be peculiar to the Lower Silurian;
Actinospongia, Goniospongia, and *Perispongia*
to the oolite ; and *Hemispongia, Thalamospon-
gia, Meandrospongia, Retispongia, Cœlopty-
chium, Pleurostoma, Turonia,* with many others,
to the chalk. The curious genus *Cliona,* which

possesses the remarkable power of excavating burrows for itself in shells and other calcareous bodies, is found in most of the secondary and tertiary formations, and is sufficiently abundant along the shores of the existing ocean. Since, however, we are still by no means certain as to what constitutes a genus among recent Sponges, it is evident that even greater difficulties must attend our investigations among extinct forms, and hence, any tabular arrangement showing the successive appearance and relative distribution of these " genera " seems to us, at present, premature.

11. **Affinity to Foraminifera.**—The nature of the relationship between the Sponges and amœbiform Rhizopods has been already alluded to. Recently, Dr. J. E. Gray has described, under the names of *Carpenteria* and *Dujardinia,* two remarkable attached forms of *Protozoa,* presenting characters intermediate between those of the *Spongidæ* and *Foraminifera.* Both of these are furnished with conical calcareous shells, composed of an aggregation of elongated chambers disposed in a spiral, the orifice of the last-formed chamber being placed at the apex of the entire shell. In *Carpenteria,* the interior of the chambers " is filled with a fleshy sponge-like body, strengthened by numerous minute, simple, pin-shaped and fusiform smooth spicula placed in bundles." In both of these organisms the entire shell is pierced with very many, minute, circular perforations.

CHAPTER V.

THALASSICOLLIDÆ.

1. External characters. — 2. Organisation. — 3. Acanthometra.

1. **External characters.** — The group of *Thalassicollidæ* includes certain gelatinous marine animals which, though abundant in most seas, would appear to have remained altogether unnoticed until the year 1851 when Mr. Huxley first directed the attention of naturalists to the peculiarities of structure which they present. They can scarcely be said to possess any determinate form, and seem to be destitute of the power of voluntary motion, being usually found floating near the surface of the water. In size they vary from an inch downwards.

2. **Organisation.** — *Sphærozoum punctatum*, one of the most abundant of these animals, presents in many cases a somewhat ovate body constricted in the centre (*fig.* 9, *a*), and is found to consist of a transparent, colourless, gelatinous substance, destitute of structure, surrounding a large internal cavity. Enclosed in the gelatinous mass are a number of isolated, minute, "cellæ-form bodies" (*e*), each of which consists of an external membrane filled with granular contents, within which a "clear fatty-looking" nucleus may be observed.

The gelatinous mass frequently contains minute, yellow, spherical cells, these being either irregularly diffused through its substance or grouped around each of the cellæform bodies.

The cellæform bodies are often surrounded
by peculiar cylindrical spicula, terminating at
both extremities in three or four conical rays,
beset on either side with minute spine-like processes.

Fig. 9.

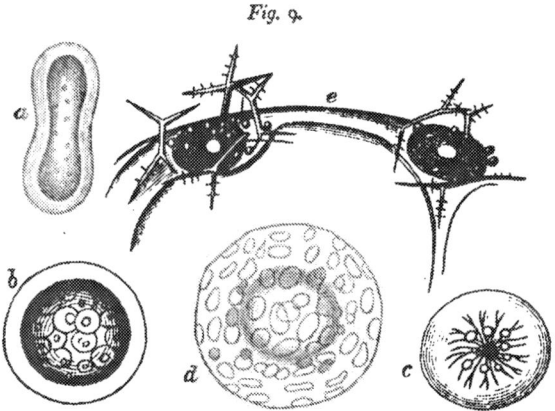

Structure of THALASSICOLLIDÆ :— *a, Sphærozoum punctatum*
(nat. size) ; *b,* variety of the same ; *c, Thalassicolla nucleata ;
d, Collosphæra Huxleyi; e,* portion of *a* (magnified), showing
two of the cellæform bodies with their coloured vesicles, nuclei,
and spicula.

In some specimens the central cavity is replaced by an aggregation of large vacuolar
spaces (*b*).

Thalassicolla proper is more constant in form
than the preceding, and is destitute of cellæform
bodies (*c*). It contains, however, the coloured vesicles above referred to ; these, associated with vacuolar spaces and very many minute dark granules,

being aggregated round a blackish body placed in
the centre of the spherical mass. The dark central body is found on examination to consist of
a strong elastic membrane, enclosing a pale
nucleus-like vesicle, embedded in a somewhat
peculiar granular substance. Numerous slender
branching "fibrils" radiate through the gelatinous body from the interior of the dark central
mass.

In *Collosphæra* the spicules are absent, but the
entire animal is enclosed in a transparent, reticulated, very brittle shell (*d*).

From the preceding account it will be evident
that the *Thalassicollidæ* differ essentially from the
other groups of *Astomatous Protozoa*, though they
at the same time present remarkable affinities to
more than one of these. Of their animal nature
no doubt can be entertained, notwithstanding the
assertion made by some that "they are referrible
rather to the Diatomaceæ," whilst others have designated them " agglomerations of organised *ra-
phides*, as it were, raised to the state of independent beings."

3. **Acanthometræ.** — The curious *Acanthometræ* of J. Müller are closely allied to the preceding. Their peculiar, siliceous, radiating spines,
which meet in the centre of the gelatinous body
and project in most cases considerably beyond
its surface, will sufficiently serve to distinguish
them (*fig.* 10). Like the *Thalassicollidæ*, the
Acanthometræ are marine, and destitute of locomotive power. In size they are more minute.
It was proposed by Müller to unite these animals

Fig. 10.

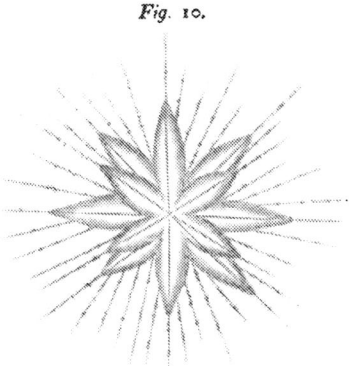

ACANTHOMETRA LANCEOLATA.

together with the *Polycystina* and *Thalassicollidæ* into a group by themselves named *Rhizopodia radiolaria.* This arrangement is indicated in the accompanying table.

TABLE

SHOWING MÜLLER'S ARRANGEMENT OF

THE THALASSICOLLIDÆ, POLYCYSTINA, AND ACANTHOMETRÆ.

RHIZOPODA RADIOLARIA.

A. RADIOLARIA SOLITARIA.
(Single.)

1. Thalassicollina.
(Animal naked: with or without siliceous spicula.)

2. Polycystina.
(Animal enclosed in a siliceous, reticulated, shelly covering.)

3. Acanthometra.
(Animal naked: with siliceous radiating spines.)

B. RADIOLARIA POLYZOA.
(Aggregated.)

1. Sphærozomidæ.
(Animal naked: with or without siliceous spicula.)

2. Collosphæridæ.
(Animal enclosed in a siliceous reticulated covering.)

CHAPTER VI.

GREGARINIDÆ.

1. Habit. — 2. Form and Structure. — 3. Development. — 4. Classification. — 5. Psorospermiæ.

1. **Habit.** — Dufour was the first to designate under the name of *Gregarinæ* a group of microscopic organisms which differ remarkably in habit from the preceding *Protozoa*, since they have hitherto been only known to occur as parasites within the bodies of other animals, more especially those belonging to the sub-kingdom *Annulosa*.

2. **Form and Structure.** — The form of the body varies, being, in most cases, more or less ovate. In many *Gregarinidæ* it is marked by clefts or strictures which, with their corresponding internal septa, divide it into two or more segments (*fig.* 11). In some, a sort of process projects from one end of the body, and this is frequently furnished at its extremity with a number of reflexed hooklets, by means of which it is supposed that these animals are enabled to attach themselves more firmly to those surfaces whereon they are usually found (*d*).

Anatomically, the *Gregarinidæ* are found to consist of a transparent membrane enclosing a mass of granular contents, in the interior of which a nucleus, surrounded by a well defined clear space, may in most cases be observed (*c, d, f*).

The *Gregarinidæ* are colourless, and would appear to possess a limited amount of locomotive power.

E

3. **Development.** — These animals have been observed to propagate by a peculiar method, to which the term "conjugating process" has been, it would seem, somewhat hastily and erroneously applied. Two *Gregarinæ* come into contact and a cyst or capsule soon forms around them both.

Fig. 11.

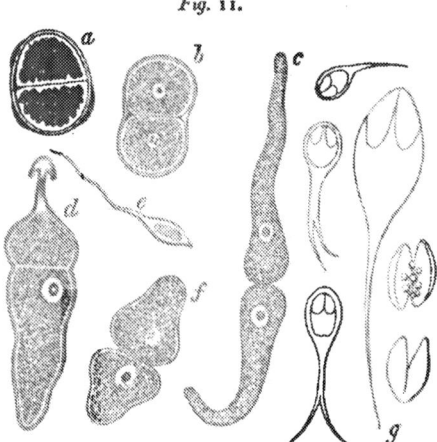

GREGARINÆ and PSOROSPERMIÆ : — *a*, cyst of *Gregarina sœnuridis*, with two cells, containing in their interior a number of pseudonaviculæ ; *b*, *Gregarina Sipunculi*, with two enclosed cells ; *c*, two *Gregarinæ sœnuridis*, adhering together by their ends ; *d*, *Gregarina Sieboldii* ; *e*, peculiar pseudonavicula (?) from abdominal cavity of Sipunculus nudus ; *f*, younger stage of *a* ; *g*, various *Psorospermiæ*.

Next, certain globular vesicles are produced in the interior of the cyst, and these become ultimately metamorphosed into peculiar bodies which have received the name of "pseudonaviculæ" (*a*, *e*, *f*).

The partition by which the two *Gregarinæ* were at first separated meanwhile disappears, the cyst bursts, and the pseudonaviculæ escaping therefrom burst in their turn, and give rise to amœbiform bodies which at length develope themselves into young *Gregarinidæ*. But the coalescence of two *Gregarinidæ* is by no means a necessary preliminary to the formation of pseudonaviculæ, since these are sometimes observed to occur within the bodies of single animals.

4. **Classification.** — The *Gregarinidæ* have been divided by Stein into three sections, viz. : —

1. *Monocystideœ.* —Simple Gregarinidæ without constrictions or internal septa.
2. *Gregarinariœ.* — Gregarinidæ with the body divided into two portions.
3. *Didimophydœ.* —Gregarinidæ with the body divided into three parts, as if resulting from the adhesion of two individuals, one from each of the preceding sections.

This, however, is merely an arbitrary division, and, if not erroneous, is certainly premature.

By some the *Gregarinidæ* have been regarded as vegetable forms ; by others, as larval stages of various *Annuloïda*. Neither of these opinions has been supported by proofs, and, upon the whole, it seems desirable, for the present at least, to view these organisms as adult members of the sub-kingdom *Protozoa*.

5. **Psorospermiæ.** — The *Psorospermiæ* are exceedingly minute parasitic creatures, occurring in great numbers both on and within the bodies of fishes. In form they are ovate, hemispherical,

or depressed, and are frequently provided with a peculiar fish-like tail (*fig.* 11, *g*). They consist of a somewhat tough external membrane, within which are two or more oblong vesicles, usually situated near the anterior extremity of the body. In addition to these a globular mass of organisable matter may often be observed. Lieberkühn has shown that, under certain circumstances, the *Psorospermiæ* may burst, when the globular mass, thus liberated, will be found to resemble the amœbiform bodies resulting from the rupture of the pseudonaviculæ above referred to. Hence it is exceedingly probable that the *Psorospermiæ* are identical with the pseudonaviculæ of true *Gregarinidæ*.

CHAPTER VII.

INFUSORIA.

1. **Nature of Infusoria.** — If water, in contact with organic matter, be exposed to the atmosphere for a few days, it will probably be found to contain, upon examination, a considerable number and variety of living beings, whose size is such as to render the majority of them invisible to the unassisted eye. These minute creatures received from the older microscopists the name of *Infusoria*, a term having reference to their frequent occurrence in most animal and vegetable infusions. Subsequently, they were investigated with great industry by Ehrenberg, who figured and described a vast number of "species" belonging to the group, all of which he arranged under two leading divisions, denominated respectively, *Rotifera* and *Polygastrica*. But the recent observations of several eminent naturalists have, however, shown

1st, That the organisation of the *Rotifera* is of a far higher nature than had been suspected by Ehrenberg, and that the true position of these animals is in the Annulose sub-kingdom; and,

2ndly, That the *Polygastrica* of Ehrenberg may be defined as a heterogeneous assemblage of

E 3

minute (in most cases, organised) beings, chiefly consisting of

    A. Rhizopoda;
    B. Unicellular and other Algæ;
    C. Embryonic forms; and, lastly,
    D. True Infusoria.

The true nature of many of the *Infusoria* proper is still a disputed question.

According to Dujardin, their bodies are composed of a gelatinous substance, similar to that which we find among the *Rhizopoda*. By Siebold, Meyen, Kölliker, and others, they have been regarded as unicellular animals; a view of their nature which certainly does not appear to be confirmed by the examination of the more highly organised forms. Agassiz, on the other hand, has endeavoured to get rid of the entire group of *Infusoria* by assigning higher positions in the animal kingdom to those of its members whose non-embryonic nature would seem to be fully established.

In the midst of so many conflicting opinions, the following course has seemed to us most worthy of adoption.

Combining the results of our own recent observations with those of the more elaborate investigations of Claparède, Lachmann, and others, we shall, with some limitations, adopt the views of the last-mentioned authors, and define the *Infusoria* as *Animals belonging to the department of Protozoa, provided with a mouth and rudimentary digestive apparatus; their bodies usually consisting of three distinct layers, the outer of which is, in most cases, furnished with a variable number of cilia.*

2. Example of the group: Vorticella.

— A good example of the true *Infusoria* is furnished by *Vorticella,* a large and well-known form, found plentifully on the roots of duckweed and other similar situations. A group of these elegant organisms, when placed under the microscope, presents the appearance of a number of bell-shaped vases, each of which surmounts the extremity of a slender pedicle or stalk (*fig.* 12, *a*).

Fig. 12.

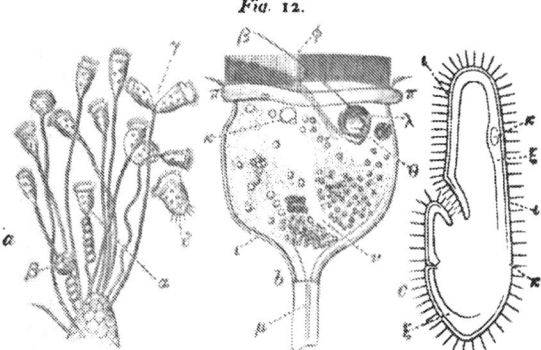

Structure of Vorticella, &c. : — *a,* group of *Vorticella ne-bulifera,* showing at α, a Vorticella spirally contracted on its stalk ; β, another form, with its cilia retracted ; γ, a third form, undergoing fissiparous division ; δ, a detached Vorticella bud, furnished with a posterior circlet of cilia ; — *b,* upper portion of *Vorticella campanula* (very much magnified) ; φ, commencement of ciliary spiral ; π, peristome , λ, lumen of œsophagus ; β, bent bristle situated in the vestibulum ; θ, one of the stronger cilia which arise in front of the mouth ; κ, contractile vesicle ; ν, band-like nucleus ; ι, cuticle ; μ, contractile filament of stem forming apical prolongation of contractile layer ; — *c,* diagrammatic section of *Paramecium,* showing ι, cuticle bearing the cilia ; κ, κ, contractile vesicles contained in the parenchyma of the body, ξ.

If one of these vase-like bodies (b) be carefully
examined, its edge is seen to be surrounded by a
projecting rim or border, which has received the
name of 'peristome' (π). Within the latter is
placed the 'disk,' the outer edge of which is
provided with one or more circlets of cilia (ϕ).
The peristome itself is not furnished with these
appendages. The mouth is placed in a small
opening situated near the edge of the disk,
between it and the peristome. The disk, which is
separated from the peristome by an intervening
furrow, forms the upper surface of a peculiar process termed the 'rotatory organ,' which the
animal has the power of retracting deeply into the
interior of the body, over which latter a covering
is then formed by the contraction of the peristome. The cilia with which the outer edge of the
disk is furnished are arranged in a spiral line.
This spiral commences a little to the right of the
oral orifice, above which it proceeds towards
the left, and, after performing one or more revolu-
tions round the edge of the disk, descends into the
'vestibulum' or commencement of the digestive
apparatus. In addition to the oral orifice, the
vestibulum is provided with a lateral aperture
which would appear to discharge the function of
an anus. Between the anus and the mouth
springs a stiff bent 'bristle' (β), which usually
projects beyond the edge of the peristome. From
the vestibulum a short tube called the 'œsophagus' leads to a wider portion of the digestive
canal which has been termed the 'pharynx.'
The latter is fusiform in shape, being truncated at
its lower extremity, which hangs down into the interior of the body, forming an abrupt termination

to the simple alimentary apparatus. It should also be mentioned that the spiral line commenced by the circlet of cilia is continued by the vestibulum and œsophagus, the longitudinal axis of which may be considered as nearly parallel to the plane of the ciliary disk. The position of the pharynx, on the other hand, is perpendicular to this plane, so as almost to correspond with the general axis of the body.

Externally, the *Vorticella* is invested with a thin membranous integument or 'cuticle' (ι), within which is placed the 'parenchyma of the body' sometimes known as the 'cortical layer.' In the substance of the latter may usually be seen the 'contractile vesicle' (κ), which lies close beneath the cuticle, near the anterior extremity of the body. In contact with the parenchymatous layer may also be detected the peculiar band-like body termed the 'nucleus' (ν), the position of which would seem to vary in different individuals. The 'stalk' of the *Vorticella* consists of a tubular prolongation of the cuticle, having its longitudinal axis traversed by a peculiar contractile filament (μ), which is regarded by some observers as the produced apex of a special contractile layer, distinct from the 'parenchyma of the body.'

By the rapid motion of its vibratile cilia the *Vorticella* is enabled to create currents in the surrounding water, by means of which any alimentary particles that may be floating therein are brought into the neighbourhood of the vestibulum. Some of these are rejected, whilst others are quickly propelled through the ciliated œsophagus into the pharynx, where they usually remain until a sufficient number become aggregated into a single morsel. The latter then quits the alimentary apparatus and is passed into the interior of the body, to the posterior extremity of which it runs, and then, turning upwards, rises on that side which is opposite the pharynx. For some time after the morsel has passed from the pharynx it retains the fusiform shape which it had acquired therein, but when, changing its course, it commences to turn upwards, it becomes somewhat globular in form. As soon as this is the case it ceases to have any separate motion of its own, and takes part in a general rotatory movement which is shared by the entire contents of the interior of the body, the nucleus alone (according to Lachmann) being exempted. The morsel, after making one or more circuits within the body, at length arrives in the neighbourhood of the anus through which it passes into the vestibulum. The final removal of the indigestible remains of the food is effected by means of the strong non-vibratile cilia which arise in front of the mouth, and it is not improbable that these (which must not be confounded with the vibratile cilia belonging to the spiral) are also employed in guarding the commencement of the alimentary apparatus from the ingress of coarse or adventitious particles, which might otherwise obstruct the entrance of the œsophagus.

Though usually fixed, the *Vorticella* is sometimes observed to detach itself and swim slowly about in the surrounding water; it has also the power, when alarmed, of contracting its stalk into a series of spiral folds, and of again causing it to resume its erect position, both of these movements being performed with great rapidity.

3. **Classification.** — Of the numerous me-
thods of arranging the *Infusoria* which, at different times, have been proposed, those of Ehrenberg, Dujardin, and Claparède appear to be most
worthy of attention. All these classifications must,
however, be regarded as premature, since we know
so little of the life-history of these animals that
it is by no means improbable that many apparently distinct species are nothing more than
transitional conditions of more adult forms. It is
now many years since it was satisfactorily demonstrated by Cohn, that at least *eight* of Ehrenberg's
genera were merely so many different stages in the
development of *one* of the lower Algæ. Hence,
in the following account of the *Infusoria*, it will be
desirable to confine ourselves to the description of
those more important characteristic features which
have been made the subject of renewed and careful investigation, directing attention, as we proceed, to those members of the group, in which
such characteristics may most readily be observed.

4. **Size.** — The *Infusoria* vary considerably in
size, the greater number being invisible without
the assistance of the microscope. Thus the ave-
rage length of the body of *Vorticella*, exclusive of
the stalk, may be estimated at ·003 of an inch.
Stentor (*fig.* 13, *a*), which is, perhaps, the largest
of all *Infusoria*, attains a length of ·04 of an inch,
whilst others are so minute as to present the appearance of mere moving points under the higher
powers of the most improved instruments. But,
since the true nature of these last can be judged
of only by analogy, it seems probable that they
ought rather to be regarded as vegetable monads,

or embryos, either of higher animals or true *In-fusoria.*

5. **Form and Structure.** — In outward form the *Infusoria* may be said to vary indefinitely, all being, however, more or less rounded (*figs.* 13 and 14). The presence of a simple spirally contractile stalk is especially characteristic of the true

Fig. 13.

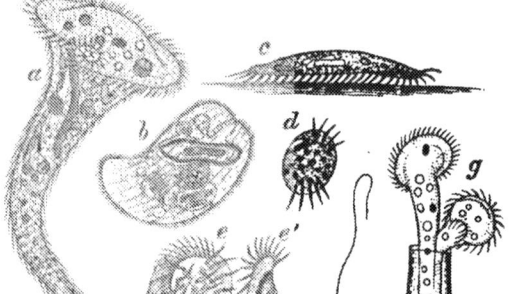

Various forms of INFUSORIA : — *a, Stentor Mülleri; b, Chilodon cucullulus; c, Oxytricha gibba; d, Aspidisca lynceus; e, Euplotes patella* (under view) ; *e'*, the same (side view) ; *f, Peranema globulosa; g, Vaginicola crystallina.*

Vorticellæ; in other stalked forms, the pedicle is either rigid as in *Epistylis,* or branched as in *Carchesium* and *Zoothamnium. Vaginicola (fig.* 13, *g*) has the body protected by a membranous or

horny 'carapace,' within which the animal can re-
treat when alarmed; and, in some cases, additional
protection would seem to be afforded by a valve
placed obliquely across the upper end of this
sheath (*fig.* 14, *a*). In *Lagotia* (*b*) the rotatory
organ terminates in a pair of wide ciliated lobes
which are seldom seen at rest during the life of
the animal. In *Ophrydium*, the most anomalous,

Fig. 14.

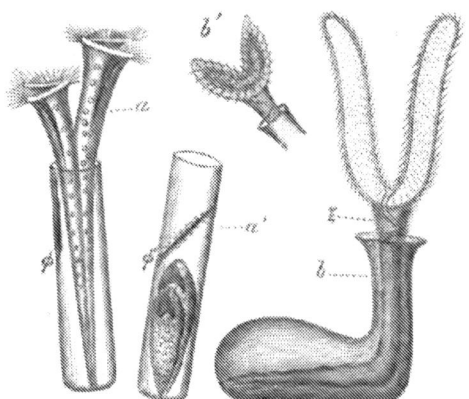

Marine INFUSORIA : — *a*, *Vaginicola valvata*, showing animal
extended and valve (φ) raised ; *a'*, the same, showing animal
contracted within its sheath and valve (φ') shut down ; — *b*,
Lagotia viridis, showing rotatory organ ꝣ ; *b'*, young animal of
preceding.

perhaps, of all the true *Infusoria*, the several
animalcules, though sometimes found detached,
are more frequently embedded in the interior of a
greenish gelatinous substance, which sometimes
occurs in masses of such extent as to have been

mistaken for frog's spawn, to which, in consistence, it bears some resemblance.

Anatomically, the bodies of most *Infusoria* may
be regarded as consisting essentially of three distinct structures, viz. : —

1. The cuticle or integument ("pellicula" of
   Carter) on which are borne the cilia and
   other locomotive apparatus (*fig.* 12, c—c);
2. The cortical layer or parenchyma of the body
   ("diaphane" of Carter) (ξ); and
3. The chyme mass, abdominal cavity, or interior of the body (sarcode or "abdominal
   mucus" of Carter), within which the particles
   of the food rotate.

It is not certain whether the carapace, with
which some *Infusoria* are provided, be distinct
from the cuticle properly so called. We have
already seen how, in *Vaginicola* and its allies, it
is so far separated from the rest of the body as to
act the part of a protective sheath.

Of the above structures, the second alone possesses any contractile power.

In those *Infusoria* which are attached, e. g.
Vorticella, the free extremity of the body which
bears the ciliary disk is termed "anterior," the
end remote from this being said to be "posterior." The term "ventral" is usually applied
to that side of the body on which the mouth is
placed.

6. **Digestive apparatus.** — In all those *Infusoria* whose animal nature has been placed above
suspicion the presence of a mouth must be regarded as universal, though the position of this
organ varies considerably among the different

members of the group. The mouth is often surrounded with cilia. These cilia, as we have seen in the case of *Vorticella*, are usually continued into the œsophagus, though the latter would seem to be in some cases destitute of these appendages. In most *Infusoria* the œsophagus presents the appearance of an open tube, freely hanging down into the cavity of the body; but in some of these animals it is completely collapsed, and it is only in *Vorticella* and a few of its allies that it has been observed to widen below into a pharynx. Recently, however, it has been proved by the observations of Lieberkühn, that in *Trachelius* and *Loxodes* the œsophagus is continued into a peculiar ramified canal. In other *Infusoria* it is altogether wanting, and in these the alimentary apparatus consists merely of a mouth leading into a cavity excavated through the parenchyma of the body. In *Chilodon* and *Nassula*, the interior of the œsophagus is provided with a number of peculiar rod-like "teeth" arranged in the form of a cylinder (*fig.* 13, *b*). Besides the oral orifice, many *Infusoria* are provided with an anus, which in *Stentor, Vorticella,* and certain of their allies, is situated not far from the mouth, close beneath the surface of the disk, whilst in others, e. g. *Bursaria,* it is placed at the posterior extremity of the body.

7. **Contractile vesicle**. — We have already noticed in *Amœba* and *Actinophrys* the existence of certain clear spaces which occur in the substance of the body, and in which movements of contraction and dilatation have been seen to take place. Similar contractile vesicles have been observed in most of the true *Infusoria*, being usually situated in some part of the parenchyma of the body

(*fig.* 12, *κ*). In their dilated condition these vesicles would seem to be filled with a clear fluid,
which suddenly disappears when they contract.
It may, in some cases, be noticed that the vesicles
are furnished with branches or processes, and
Lachmann asserts that he has seen two such processes issue from the large contractile space of
Stentor polymorphus, the one annular, running
beneath the surface of the ciliary disk, the other
longitudinal, proceeding to the posterior extremity
of the body. When the vesicle contracts, both of
these "vessels" suddenly expand, the longitudinal
vessel, in particular, being seen to present numerous dilatations. At the same time two rounded
expansions make their appearance in the annular
vessel, the one being situated in the neighbourhood of the anus, the other lying close to the
œsophagus, on the ventral surface of the body.
When the contractile vesicle reappears, both of
these vessels gradually decrease, "apparently without any contraction of their own." In healthy specimens of *Bursaria*, *Ophryoglena*, and *Paramecium*, the contractile vesicles, together with their
associated vessels, assume a peculiar stellate form.
These and other similar appearances, observed in
the bodies of various *Infusoria*, are supposed by
some to present us with what may, perhaps, be
termed a rudimentary apparatus of circulation.

It seems proper to distinguish the above contractile vesicles from certain other clear spaces
which have received from Dujardin the name of
"vacuoles." These may make their appearance
in any part of the interior of the body, and are
usually observable within a short period after food
has been swallowed. They may readily be known

from true 'vesicles' by the variations which continually occur in their size, number, and position.

8. **Nucleus, &c.**--Most, if not all, of the *Infusoria* are provided with one or more central solid particles or 'nuclei,' the presence of which we have already stated to be more or less characteristic of the *Protozoa*. The nucleus varies in position, being in most cases attached to some part of the parenchyma of the body. It varies also both in form and structure. Thus in Vorticella and *Stentor* it is elongated, band-like, consisting of an external membrane filled with granular contents, whilst in *Ophryoglena* (according to Lieberkühn) it is ovate, and destitute of any apparent structure. In other *Infusoria* it may be either round (*Oxytricha*), reniform (*Loxodes*), shaped like a horse-shoe (*Euplotes*), or spiral (as in some species of *Stentor*). Sometimes, though rarely, it is branched. In colour it is usually pale yellow.

In the granular contents of some nuclei a clear space or cavity is observable, within which a smaller body termed the 'nucleolus' is placed. In other cases it occurs on the exterior of the same organ. Lieberkühn describes the nucleolus of *Ophryoglena* as minute, globular, structureless, and firmly attached to the surface of the ovate nucleus. But in *Chilodon*, the centre of the nucleolus is marked by a transparent dot.

A bright coloured particle (usually red), termed the 'pigment-spot,' is found in the bodies of many *Infusoria*. In some it is altogether destitute of structure, in others it is made up of a number of exceedingly minute granules.

F

In *Ophryoglena flavicans* a remarkable body termed the "watch-glass-like organ" has been recently observed by Lieberkühn. It is colourless, transparent, homogeneous, and immovable, with its convex side turned towards the pigment spot, whilst its concave side is directed towards the point of the head. It has also been detected in *Bursaria flava*. Its use (as also that of the pigment spot) is unknown.

9. **Urticating organs.** — In the cortical layer of *Bursaria*, certain peculiar fusiform bodies or 'trichocysts' have been detected, and from these Prof. Allman states that he has observed the emission of minute filaments which bear some resemblance to the urticating organs of the fresh-water polype. They occur, also, in other *Infusoria*.

10. **Locomotive organs.** — In by far the greater number of *Infusoria* locomotion is effected by the vibratile movements of the peculiar hair-like appendages usually denominated cilia. The cause of these movements is at present unknown, nor is it certain whether they are dependent upon volition. The cilia vary in position and mode of arrangement among the several members of the group. Thus, in *Enchelys* they are scattered, apparently without order, over the entire surface of the body; in *Vorticella* and *Vaginicola* they are confined to the neighbourhood of the anterior extremity, whilst in *Paramecium* and its allies they are disposed in a series of regular rows, parallel to one another. In other *Infusoria* they either surround the entire margin of the flattened body, or encircle it in the form of an oblique

spiral. In *Trichodina* there is a crown of cilia on the back, in addition to which a peculiar undulatory membrane, richly furnished with these minute organs, occurs on the ventral surface of the body.

In form the cilia may be described as elongated, broader at the base than at the tip, being usually somewhat flattened. They vary in length from ·02 to about ·00005 of an inch. Their motion is mostly uniform, each of the cilia bending in rapid succession from its base to its point, and returning immediately to its original condition: sometimes these movements suddenly cease, but after a moment's pause they are again resumed either in the same or in an opposite direction. From their minute size the cilia are often difficult of detection. Their presence, in many cases, can hardly be ascertained until their motion has very much slackened, or it may be indirectly inferred from the agitation of floating particles caused by the currents which are excited in the surrounding water.

By means of these cilia, the *Infusoria* move rapidly about in the water wherein they are found, and it is curious to observe how, when a number are confined to a small portion of that fluid, they rarely seem to come into collision with one another or any obstacles which may be placed in their way.

Besides the true cilia, other appendages, of apparently similar nature, but larger size, are met with among many *Infusoria*. Such, for example, are the 'setæ' or ciliary bristles of *Oxytricha* (*fig.* 13, *c*), the 'uncini' (hooks) and 'styles' of *Euplotes* (*e, e'*), and the 'flagelliform filaments' of *Peranema* (*f*). The latter may be described as long filamentous prolongations, proceeding from the anterior extremity of the body, their terminations only being capable of performing vibratory movements. But there is reason to infer that many of the organisms in which they occur are, in all probability, members of the vegetable kingdom.

All the above appendages are properly to be regarded as elongated processes of the cuticular layer. It has been asserted by some observers that each of the cilia arises from the apex of a four-sided prism. But further observation on this point is necessary.

The contractile movements which the stalk of *Vorticella* undergoes have been described in our account of that Infusorium.

11. **Development.** — Propagation is effected among the *Infusoria* by

a. Fission,
b. Gemmation,
c. Encystation, and
d. True reproduction (i. e. by ova and spermatozoa)?

Of these the three first tend to separate the individual into a number of seemingly independent beings or 'zoöids,' while the fourth method gives rise to new individuals. For an individual (in Zoölogy) is equal to "the total result of the development of a simple ovum."

a. Multiplication by the method of fissiparous division is of frequent occurrence. It may be either longitudinal (*Vorticella*), or transverse (*Stentor*), or either indifferently (*Chilodon*, *Euplotes*, *Paramecium*). It is usually stated that

the process of separation first commences in the
nucleus, but this is incorrect, since in some cases
its division into two parts is not effected until
that of the body is nearly complete, or it may
happen that fission of the nucleus is not partici-
pated in by the body as a whole.

b. Gemmation (or the development of buds)
takes place far less frequently than fission. It is
best seen in *Vorticella.* Here a bud is formed
(usually near the posterior extremity of the body)
by the expansion of a portion of the cortical layer.
This at first derives its nutriment by means of a
diverticulum or prolongation proceeding from the
digestive cavity of the parent animal. At length
this connection is interrupted, the bud becomes
furnished with a posterior circlet of cilia, by the
aid of which it finally detaches itself and swims
freely about in the surrounding water (*fig.* 12, δ).
It should, however, be borne in mind that the difference between fission and gemmation is more
apparent than real, and in many cases it is impossible to distinguish the one from the other.

c. Some *Infusoria*, previously to undergoing fission, become coated with a secretion of gelatinous
matter which gradually hardens so as to enclose
the body in a 'cyst.' In other cases, peculiar
vesicular bodies become formed in the interior of
such cysts, through which they finally burst, and,
becoming ruptured at the apex, give exit to the
embryos contained in their interior. But it would
appear, from recent observations, that the previous formation of a cyst is by no means necessa-
rily antecedent to the production of the vesicles
in question.

According to Stein, the process of encystation

is sometimes followed by a remarkable succession of phenomena, which have been thus described by their discoverer, as they occur in the case of *Vorticella microstoma* (*fig.* 15). An old *Vorticella* loses or retracts its cilia, becomes encysted (*a*) and finally drops off its stalk (*b*). The cyst may either burst and discharge its contents

Fig. 15.

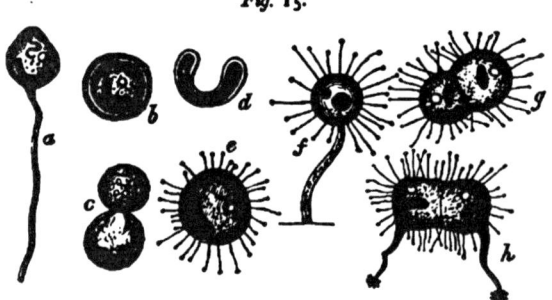

Development of VORTICELLA MICROSTOMA : — *a*, old *Vorticella* in its encysted state, the nucleus and contractile vesicle being visible within the body ; *b*, the same, detached from its stalk ; *c*, cyst discharging its contents ; *d*, the band-like nucleus, isolated ; *e*, *Acineta* form of encysted *Vorticella* ; *f*, stalked *Acineta* (= *Podophyra*) form of the same ; *g*, two *Acineta* forms in a state of conjugation ; *h*, two *Podophyra* forms in the same condition.

in the manner already indicated (*c*), or become changed into an " *Acineta* form " (*e*). The latter may subsequently develop a stalk, so as to assume the appearance of a " *Podophyra* " (*f*). In either instance, the band-like nucleus becomes transformed into a peculiar ovate body, the narrow end of which is provided with a circlet of vibratile cilia, whilst a mouth leading into an internal cavity soon becomes formed at its opposite extremity; at the same time a nucleus and contractile vesicle may be observed in its interior. Ultimately the ovate body escapes through a rupture formed in the wall of the cyst, which soon after closes, and after a while a new nucleus is produced in its interior, which in its turn may become transformed in the same manner as its predecessor.

Relations somewhat similar to those which connect *Vorticella* and *Acineta* have been affirmed by Haime to exist between *Aspidisca* (or *Trichoda*) (*fig.* 13, *d*) and *Oxytricha* (*c*).

If these statements be admitted as true, it follows that important modifications will be thereby effected in our views as to what constitutes a " genus " or " species " among the *Infusoria;* since they would appear to show that '*Acineta*' and *Podophyra,* usually considered to be distinct genera, are rather to be regarded as intermediate or transitional forms produced by the metaphormosis of encysted *Vorticellæ.* But the conclusions of Stein have recently been altogether rejected by Lachmann and others, who assert that in none of his observations did he take sufficient care to isolate the specimens submitted to examination.

It sometimes happens that two or more Infusoria cohere together, but in an imperfect manner, a line of demarcation being always observable between them (*fig.* 15, *g* and *h*). To this union (the object of which has not yet been ascertained) the term "conjugation" is often improperly applied.

d. Under the head of *true reproduction* the following series of changes, recently observed in *Paramecium* by Balbiani, would seem to be deserving of mention. Two *Paramecia* adhere toge-

ther, their mouths being closely applied to one
another, and in this condition they move rapidly
through the water wherein they are confined.
Next, the nucleolus of each undergoes a considerable increase in size, and assumes the form of an
ovate capsule striated on its surface. It then
divides into two or four parts which increase independently of one another, and form a number of
secondary capsules. Meanwhile the nucleus also
enlarges, becoming at the same time rounder,
wider, and softer in consistence; a number of
transparent spherical bodies are formed in its interior, within each of which an obscure central point
may be observed. Sometimes the nucleus breaks
up into fragments, previous to the formation of the
spherical bodies. After a certain period has been
permitted to elapse, a transfer is effected by the
two conjoined *Paramecia* of one or more of their
secondary capsules, which pass through the closely
appressed mouths from the body of one into that
of the other. But this does not hinder the further
increase of the capsules in size, which still con-
tinues after their transference has taken place, one
only arriving at maturity at the same time. Five
or six days after copulation minute rounded germs
make their appearance; these for a time remain
attached to the body of the parent animal by
means of the suckers with which they are provided. At length they detach themselves, lose
their suckers, acquire a mouth in their stead, and,
becoming furnished with vibratile cilia, take on
the aspect of adult *Paramecia*.

Such are the facts as stated by M. Balbiani.
He explains them by regarding the nucleus as an
ovary, its contents as ovules, and each of the

secondary capsules as a testis. The transference of the capsules is then an act of fecundation, and dissection of these bodies when fully developed would seem to corroborate this view, since they are found to contain numerous minute fusiform bodies, the extremities of which are so fine as to be almost invisible. These are said to be spermatozoa.

12. **Distribution.** — The *Infusoria* are very abundantly distributed over most parts of the globe, nor does there appear to be any remarkable difference, either in aspect or organisation, between the forms of temperate and tropical climes. They are found plentifully in ponds, lakes, rivers, salt marshes and the sea itself, some species, e. g. *Chilodon cucullulus,* being common to both fresh and salt water. They occur also in many artificial infusions, and there can be little doubt that several of these animals have been occasionally met with as internal parasites. Those who require *Infusoria* for microscopic examination may, without much difficulty, obtain most of the more remarkable forms, by searching for them diligently in suitable localities, the exact nature of which can only be learned by experience. Thus, the muddy sediment at the bottom of pools may be examined for such species as avoid the light, whilst others, on the contrary, are obtainable only by skimming the surface of the water. Careful inspection of the stems and roots of sub-aquatic plants will often reveal the presence of *Vorticella, Vaginicola, Stentor,* and other attached forms. The last-mentioned of these is almost visible to the naked eye, and the practised observer soon

learns to recognise the appearance presented by
the aggregated colonies of *Vorticella* or *Epistylis.*

There are no true fossil *Infusoria,* the organisms
usually designated by this name being either *Foraminifera, Polycystina,* or *Diatomaceæ.*

13. **Noctiluca.**—Certain of the marine *Infusoria* are phosphorescent, contributing, along with
other animals, to impart a luminous appearance
to the sea-water wherein they abound.   But this
remarkable property is possessed in a much more
eminent degree by *Noctiluca,* an organism whose

Fig. 16.

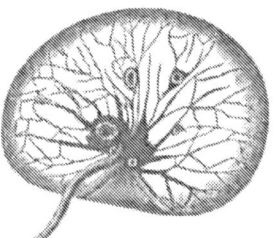

NOCTILUCA MILIARIS.

true position in the animal kingdom has long
been much misunderstood.   The simplicity of its
organisation shows it to belong to the *Protozoa;*
and, since it is provided with a distinct mouth, it
ought probably to be regarded as an aberrant
member of the group *Infusoria.* Its structure has
been of late years investigated by Quatrefages, and
Krohn, and still more recently by Mr. Huxley.
In form it is nearly globular, presenting on one
side a ' hilus,' or groove, from the anterior extre-

mity of which issues a peculiar curved stalk or appendage, marked by transverse lines, which would seem to be made use of as an organ of locomotion. Near the base of this 'tentacle' is placed the mouth, provided on one side with a tooth-like projection. The mouth leads into an 'œsophagus,' from the bottom of which a delicate flickering filament or 'cilium' is sometimes protruded. The œsophagus passes into a dilatable digestive cavity which is supposed by Mr. Huxley to be connected with a small funnel-shaped depression or 'anal aperture' situated in the midst of a flattened space behind the mouth. An oval 'nucleus,' rather less than ·002 of an inch in length, lies in front of the digestive cavity. The body of *Noctiluca* is invested by a rather firm membrane, destitute of cilia, beneath which occurs a gelatinous layer richly furnished with minute granules. From this layer arises a network of delicate granular 'fibrils,' which unite to form coarser fibres as they proceed towards the centre of the body, until finally they reach the nucleus and digestive cavity. The diameter of *Noctiluca* varies from ·04 to ·01 of an inch. It is, perhaps, the most frequent source of the *diffused* luminosity of the sea in temperate climes, the light which it emits being, as it were, the combined result of a rapid succession of vivid scintillations.

Noctiluca multiplies by spontaneous fission. Within the body of this animal Busch observed the existence of certain brown masses, containing granules in their interior. It is not certain whether these were true ova or merely the result of a process of gemmation. In other *Noctilucæ* the same observer detected peculiar germ-like bodies,

each furnished with an obtuse process. These
germs were also met with in a free condition, and
their development was traced up to a certain point,
after which Busch was obliged to discontinue his
investigations.

In the same situations as *Noctiluca*, Busch further
discovered numerous transparent gelatinous bodies,
of similar size and appearance, and possessing, in
many cases, phosphorescent properties, though not
provided with radiating fibres, or locomotive appendage. These bodies were almost destitute of
structure, but on a portion of their surface there
usually occurred several remarkable yellowish processes, either rounded or tapering to a point, containing in their interior minute spherical granules.
The nature of these problematical organisms presents a subject for future inquiry.

NOTE ON 'ACINETA FORMS.'

IT seems proper to conclude, with Lachmann, that these organisms are not, as was formerly supposed, Rhizopods allied to *Actinophrys*, nor yet again metamorphosed conditions of *Vorticellæ*, but that they rather constitute a distinct group of *Infusoria*, to which the term 'polystome' might, without objection, be perhaps applied. For each of the radiating filaments (*fig.* 15, *e*) with which the *Acinetæ* are provided is, in truth, a retractile tube, susceptible of elongation to a remarkable extent, and furnished at its extremity with an adherent disk. With the aid of these unique organs an *Acineta* is enabled, not only to seize and retain its more active prey, but also to imbibe the nutrient particles contained in the body of the latter, by a peculiar method of suction. When the size of the prey is considerable, this process has been observed to occupy several hours. With the exception of the above-mentioned mouths, no other aperture has been hitherto discovered in the bodies of these animals.

BIBLIOGRAPHY OF THE PROTOZOA.

RHIZOPODA.

a. AMŒBA, AND ITS ALLIES.

AUERBACH.—'Ueber die Einzelligkeit der Amœben.' Zeitschrift für Wissenschaftliche Zoologie, 1855.

KÖLLIKER.—'Das Sonnenthierchen, Actinophrys sol.' Zeitschr. f. Wiss. Zool., 1849, and Quarterly Journal of Microscopical Science, 1853.

BAILEY.—'Observations on a newly discovered Animalcule.' American Journal of Science and Arts, 1853.

Also: CLAPARÀDE, Müller's Archiv, 1854, and Annals of Natural History, 1855; WESTON, Quart. Journ. Micr. Sci., 1856; and several treatises on the Infusoria, more especially those of DUJARDIN, LACHMANN, and CLAPARÀDE.

b. FORAMINIFERA; GENERAL CHARACTERS.

SCHULTZE. — 'Ueber den Organismus der Polythalamien (Foraminiferen) nebst Bemerkungen über die Rhizopoden im Allgemeinen,' 1854.

WILLIAMSON. — 'On the Recent Foraminifera of Great Britain,' 1858.

Appended to this work, which contains figures and descriptions of the more important varieties of all the British species of Foraminifera, will be found a very complete bibliography of the entire group.

c. FORAMINIFERA; STRUCTURE OF THE SHELL.

CARPENTER. — 'Researches on the Foraminifera.' Philosophical Transactions, 1856–7.

CARTER.—' On the Form and Structure of Operculina Arabica.' Ann. Nat. Hist., 1852.

WILLIAMSON.—Various papers published in Quart. Journ. Micr. Sci.

d. FORAMINIFERA ; FOSSIL FORMS.

EHRENBERG.—' Ueber den Grünsand und seine Erläuterung des Organischen Lebens.' Abhandlungen der Konigl. Akademie der Wissenschaften zu Berlin, 1855.

EGGER.—' Die Foraminiferen der Miocän-Schichten bei Ortenburg in Nieder-Bayern,' 1858.

PICTET.—' Traité de Paléontologie,' 1857 ; and the 'Cours Elémentaires de Paléontologie,' and ' Prodrome de Paléontologie,' of D'ORBIGNY.

Other memoirs are indicated in the bibliography appended to the monograph of Williamson, above referred to.

POLYCYSTINA AND THALASSICOLLIDÆ.

MÜLLER, J.—' Ueber die Thalassicollen, Polycystinen und Acanthometren des Mittelmeeres.' Ab. d. K. Akad. Berlin., 1858, and Quart. Journ. Micr. Sci., 1856.

HUXLEY.—' On Thalassicolla.' Ann. Nat. Hist., 1851.

For information on the fossil Polycystinæ see EHRENBERG, 'Mikrogeologie,' 1854; Ab. d. K. Akad. Berlin, 1846-7, and Ann. Nat. Hist., 1847.

SPONGIDÆ.

BOWERBANK.—' On the Anatomy and Physiology of the Spongiadæ :' Phil. Trans., 1859. ' On the Vital Powers of the Spongiadæ :' Reports of the British Association, 1856-7; and other papers in Ann. Nat. Hist., 1841-2-5; and Quart. Journ. Micr. Sci., 1859.

HUXLEY.—'On the Anatomy of the genus Tethya.' Ann. Nat. Hist., 1851.

JOHNSTON.—' History of British Sponges and Lithophytes,' 1842.

Also: CARTER, Ann. Nat. Hist., 1848-9-54-7 ; LIEBERKÜHN, Müller's Archiv, 1856-7, and Ann. Nat. Hist., 1856 ; DOBIE, Goodsir's Annals of Anatomy and Physiology, 1852 ; HANCOCK, Ann. Nat. Hist., 1849 ; MORRIS, do. do. ; OWEN, Transactions of Zoological Society of London, 1841 ; GRAY, Ann. Nat. Hist., 1858. An account of the older memoirs on

Sponges will be found in Dr. Johnston's work, cited above. With reference to the fossil Spongidæ, the following papers may be consulted:—BOWERBANK, 'On the Siliceous Bodies of the Chalk, Greensand and Oolite,' Transactions of Geological Society of London, 1841; J. T. SMITH, 'On the Ventriculidæ of the Chalk,' Ann. Nat. Hist., 1847–8. See also PICTET, 'Traité de Paléontologie,' 1857; and the paleontological treatises of D'ORBIGNY, already alluded to.

GREGARINIDÆ (INCLUDING PSOROSPERMIÆ).

KÖLLIKER.—'Beiträge zur Kenntniss niederer Thiere.' Zeitschr. f. wiss. Zool., 1848.

LIEBERKÜHN.—'Ueber die Psorospermien.' Müller's Archiv, 1854.

Also BRUCH, Zeitschr. f. wiss. Zool., 1850; DUFOUR, Annales des Sciences Naturelles, 1828; FRANTZIUS, 'Observationes quædam de Gregarinis,' 1846; HENLE, Müller's Archiv, 1845; LEIDY, Transactions of American Philosophical Society, 1851; LEYDIG, Müller's Archiv, 1851; MÜLLER, ibid., 1841; ROBIN' 'Histoire Naturelle des Végétaux Parasites,' 1853; STEIN, Müller's Archiv, 1848.

INFUSORIA.

EHRENBERG. — 'Die Infusionsthiere als volkommene Organismen,' 1838.

DUJARDIN. — 'Infusoires,' 1841.

STEIN. — 'Infusionsthiere auf ihre Entwickelungsgeschichte untersucht,' 1854.

LACHMANN ET CLAPARÈDE. — 'Études sur les Infusoires et les Rhizopodes,' Mémoires de l'Institut National Genevois, 1858; also, Müller's Archiv, 1856, and Ann. Nat. Hist. 1857.

COHN. — Various papers published in Zeitschr. f. wiss. Zool., 1851–3–4 and 7.

See also the memoirs of AUERBACH, CZERMAK, ECKER, and CIENKOWSKY, in the same journal, together with those of various writers in Ann. Nat. Hist., Ann. Sci. Nat., Müller's Archiv, and Wiegmann's Archiv. Among these may be mentioned: CARTER, Ann. Nat. Hist., 1856–9; HAIME, Ann. Sci. Nat., 1853; LIEBERKÜHN, Müller's Archiv, 1856–7, and Ann. Nat. Hist., 1856; SCHNEIDER, Müller's Archiv, 1854,

and Ann. Nat. Hist., 1854. An abstract of the contents of
Ehrenberg's work will be found in Pritchard's 'History of
Infusorial Animalcules,' and the 'Micrographic Dictionary' of
Griffith and Henfrey. Other sources of information are:
ALLMANN, Quart. Journ. Micr. Sci., 1855; BALBIANI, Comptes
Rendus, 1858, and Ann. Nat. Hist., 1858; FOCKE, 'Amtlicher
Bericht der Naturforscherversammlung zu Bremen,' 1844;
FRANTZIUS, 'Analecta ad Ophrydii versatilis historiam natu-
ralem,' 1849; KUTORGA, 'Naturgeschichte der Infusionsthiere,
vorzüglich nach Ehrenberg's Beobachtungen,' 1841; PELTIER,
L'Institut, 1836; POUCHET, Comptes Rendus, 1849, and Ann.
Nat. Hist., 1849; SCHMIDT, Froriep's Notizen, 1849; HUXLEY,
Quart. Journ. Micr. Sci., 1857; SAMUELSON, do. do.; and
the classical treatises of LEUWENHOEK, Phil. Trans., 1676; C.
F. MÜLLER, 'Animalcula Infusoria,' 1786; and WRISBERG,
'Observationum de Animalculis infusoriis satura,' &c., 1765.
Also, T. S. WRIGHT, Edinburgh New Philosophical Journal,
1858.

NOCTILUCA.

BUSCH. — 'Das Meerleuchten und die Noctiluca,' in Beobachtungen,
über Anatomie und Entwickelung einiger wirbellosen See-
thiere, 1851.

HUXLEY: — 'On the structure of Noctiluca miliaris.' Quart. Journ.
Micr. Sci., 1855.

QUATREFAGES. — 'Observations sur les Noctiluques,' Ann. Sci.
Nat., 1850, and Ann. Nat. Hist., 1853.

Also: BRIGHTWEL, Ann. Nat. Hist., 1850; GOSSE, Devonshire
Coast, p. 253, 1853; KROHN, Wiegmann's Archiv, 1852;
LESSON, Acalèphes, p. 145, 1843; PRING, Philosophical Ma-
gazine, 1849; and WEBB, Quart Journ. Micr. Sci., 1855.

QUESTIONS ON THE PROTOZOA.

1. Why is it desirable to separate Amœba and its allies from the true Infusoria ?
2. Compare Pamphagus with Amœba and Difflugia.
3. What are Psorospermiæ?
4. Describe the process of gemmation in Vorticella.
5. In addition to the true cilia, what other locomotive organs are found among the Infusoria?
6. What animal forms were included by J. Müller in the group Rhizopoda Radiolaria?
7. Mention some of the characters by which Grantia is distinguished from other Sponges.
8. How are the Polythalamia subdivided by Schultze?
9. Into what two sections may the Rhizopoda be divided? Distinguish between them.
10 Give examples of Foraminifera which occur in the primary rocks.
11. What organised beings were included among the Infusoria of Ehrenberg?
12. By what single anatomical feature may the Infusoria be distinguished from other Protozoa?
13. Distinguish Polycystina from Foraminifera.
14. Give some account of the 'aquiferous system' of the Spongidæ.
15. Describe the structure of the seed-like body of Spongilla.
16. Of what essential structures does the body of an Infusorium consist?
17. What is meant by the term 'Sarcode'?
18. State briefly what is known concerning the development of the Rhizopoda.
19. What principle guided D'Orbigny in framing his classification of the Foraminifera ?
20. To which of his groups ought Miliolina to be referred?
21. Why is his arrangement objectionable?

22. How do Acanthometræ differ from Thalassicollidæ?
23. Give some account of the mode of propagation among the Gregarinidæ.
24. Distinguish Vorticella from other stalked forms of Infusoria.
25. What is meant by the terms, 'peristome,' 'vestibulum,' 'pharynx,' and 'œsophagus,' as applied to the Infusoria?
26. In the simple form of Orbitolites, how are the segments of sarcode contained in the outermost zone connected with those of the cells belonging to the zone immediately within it?
27. Give examples of Foraminifera in which the 'shell' is not calcareous.
28. Why are Sponges regarded as members of the Animal Kingdom?
29. Describe Gregarina Sieboldii.
30. Mention some examples of Infusoria in which the digestive cavity is furnished with a second aperture.
31. Distinguish 'vacuoles' from 'contractile vesicles.'
32. What is the nature of the so called 'fossil Infusoria'?
33. What are Thalassicollidæ?
34. Of what geological period are Nummulites chiefly characteristic?
35. In what group of the Astomatous Protozoa has true reproduction been proved to occur?
36. Give examples of widely distributed Foraminifera.
37. Define the terms, 'septum,' 'septal plane, and 'peripheral margin.'
38. How is the digestive process effected in Actinophrys?
39. How in Vorticella?
40. Why ought all classifications of the Infusoria which have hitherto been proposed to be considered premature?
41. Describe the swarm spores of Spongilla.
42. Explain the mode of growth of the shell in Miliolina.
43. How is the growth of the shell supposed to take place in Orbitolites?
44. What position does the 'nucleus' occupy in the body of an Infusorium?
45. What is the position of the nucleolus?
46. What functions has Balbiani ascribed to these two organs?
47. What facts have induced him to infer that true reproduction occurs in Paramecium?
48. Describe Noctiluca miliaris.
49. Give a resumé of Stein's account of the metamorphoses of Vorticella miscrostoma.
50. What is the position of the urticating organs in Bursaria?

LIST OF ILLUSTRATIONS.

INDEX.

THE END.

Lightning Source UK Ltd.
Milton Keynes UK
04 March 2010